D0339224

THE STORIES OF YELLOWSTONE
Adventure Tales from the World's First National Park

M. MARK MILLER

TWODOT®

GUILFORD, CONNECTICUT
HELENA, MONTANA
AN IMPRINT OF ROWMAN & LITTLEFIELD

A · TWODOT® · BOOK

TwoDot is an imprint of Rowman & Littlefield

Distributed by NATIONAL BOOK NETWORK

TwoDot is a registered trademark of Rowman & Littlefield.

British Library Cataloguing-in-Publication Information available on file.

Library of Congress Cataloging-in-Publication Data available on file.

ISBN 978-0-7627-9290-0 (paperback)

∞™ The paper used in this publication meets the minimum requirements of American National Standard for Information Sciences—Permanence of Paper for Printed Library Materials, ANSI/ NISO Z39.48-1992.

Contents

CONTENTS

PREFACE

I conjured the idea for *The Stories of Yellowstone* while signing copies of my first book at Old Faithful Inn. People there told me they were looking forward to reading the classic tales in *Adventures in Yellowstone,* but they really wanted shorter stories that they could finish while driving between sights or sitting around their evening campfire. I have compiled such a book.

I collected the stories presented here for my Humanities Montana presentation, "Sidesaddles and Geysers, Women's Adventures in Early Yellowstone" and for my blog, mmarkmiller.wordpress.com. I have edited the stories to make them easy for today's readers. Longer items have been condensed to focus on dramatic stories and events. But I have been careful to retain the authors' styles, because they convey their personalities and emotions.

I am a storyteller, not a historian. I chose accounts that were well told and described interesting experiences. No doubt many of these tales contain exaggerations and embellishments, perhaps even outright fabrications. A few are just plain fiction, and those are labeled as such in their introductions.

I have focused on putting together an anthology of vivid and gripping stories about early travel to Yellowstone Park and the surrounding area and presenting them in an entertaining way. I have edited these stories to eliminate archaic style, outdated spellings, and grammatical errors. When writers called sights and geothermal features by names no longer in use, I substituted the current label whenever possible. Sometimes I retained old names, either because they added color or it wasn't possible to determine the current name. Similarly, I have corrected errors of fact concerning such things as the height of waterfalls and the distances between sites.

The stories in this book span the period from 1807, when John Colter first discovered the wonders of the Yellowstone Plateau, to the 1910s, when tourists started speeding between luxury hotels in their automobiles. The earliest stories recount mountain men's awe at geysers hurling boiling water hundreds of feet into the air and their gun battles with hostile Indians. The latest stories are set in a time when women felt comfortable taking children to the park without an adult male accompanying them.

Many people helped in the preparation of this book. I am grateful to Humanities Montana, which included me in their impressive Speakers

Bureau, thus providing much of the motivation for collecting these stories. Too many people to name assisted me, but I particularly want to thank Ann Butterfield, who read drafts and made insightful comments, and Ralph Schmidt, whose deep knowledge of Yellowstone Park and keen editor's eye kept the manuscript grammatically and factually correct. Rachel Phillips, research coordinator of the Pioneer Museum of Bozeman, graciously shared her knowledge of the museum's collection to help me choose photographs for this book. Also, thanks to the volunteers of the Pioneer Museum, who were my first audience for these stories and provided bounteous encouragement. These people made the book better, but, of course, I take full responsibility for any errors.

Finally, I want to thank my wife, Tamara Miller, for providing moral support and lots of good company.

PART 1:
MOUNTAIN MEN

INTRODUCTION

Trappers battle Indians and discover boiling fountains throwing water hundreds of feet high.

Early in the 1800s intrepid men spread throughout the Rocky Mountain West to make their fortunes in the fur trade. At first they trapped in accessible areas along major river valleys, but soon they had harvested everything on those lands and had to move into more remote areas. Beginning about 1820 they penetrated the Yellowstone Plateau. Soon most of the beaver were gone, and fashions in men's hats changed from beaver to silk. The last time mountain men held a big rendezvous to trade furs for supplies was in 1840. After the bottom fell out of the beaver trade, the mountain men dispersed. Some went back east, others headed west to the burgeoning Oregon Territory. Some were hired on as guides for wagon trains headed west and for the army. A few stayed in the mountains, subsisting by hunting, fishing, and trapping to trade for essentials. Yellowstone tourists described encountering mountain men as late as the 1880s.

Colter's Run

(1807)—John Bradbury

Indians strip a trapper naked and turn him loose to run for his life.

Although the mountain man era in Yellowstone Park had its heyday in the 1820s and 1830s, it actually began in 1807, when John Colter became the first white man to visit the area. People have told and retold John Colter's adventures with embellishments that turn him into a legendary figure like Pecos Bill and Paul Bunyan. But Colter was not a fictional character. He really did cross the plains naked after outrunning hundreds of Blackfeet warriors who were screaming for his scalp. He really was the first white man to visit what is now Yellowstone National Park. And his reports of a stinking place where springs spout steam and boiling water were greeted as fantasy and labeled "Colter's Hell."

Colter was a member of the famous Lewis and Clark Expedition that first explored the American West beginning in 1803. He came within fifty miles of what is now the park in 1806 when he accompanied William Clark on the return trip down the Yellowstone River.

Later, Colter sought permission to muster out of the Corps of Discovery so he could return upriver with a pair of trappers. After extracting a promise from the rest of the men that they wouldn't seek similar treatment, the captains acceded to his request.

Colter soon broke up with his partners, and he joined Manuel Lisa's Missouri Fur Company. In 1807 Lisa sent Colter up the Yellowstone River to make friends with the Crow Indians and bring them back to his trading post. While he was on this mission, Colter passed through parts of what is now Yellowstone National Park.

Apparently illiterate, Colter left no written accounts of his travels. But on a visit to St. Louis in 1810, Colter told his adventures to English writer and naturalist John Bradbury. In a footnote in his 1819 book, Travels in the Interior of America, *Bradbury provided this version of the story, known widely as "Colter's Run."*

Colter came to St. Louis in May, 1810, in a small canoe, from the headwaters of the Missouri, a distance of three thousand miles. I saw him on his arrival, and received from him an account of his adventures. One of these, from its singularity, I shall relate.

He trapped in company with a hunter named Potts. Aware of the hostility of the Blackfeet Indians, they set their traps at night, and took them up early in the morning, remaining concealed during the day.

They were examining their traps early one morning, in a creek about six miles from that branch of the Missouri called Jefferson's Fork, and were ascending in a canoe. Suddenly they heard a great noise, resembling the trampling of animals. But they could not ascertain the cause, as the high, perpendicular banks on each side of the river impeded their view.

Colter immediately pronounced it to be occasioned by Indians, and advised an instant retreat. Potts accused him of cowardice and insisted that the noise was caused by buffaloes. In a few minutes their doubts were removed by a party of Indians making their appearance on both sides of the creek—five or six hundred—who beckoned them to come ashore.

As retreat was now impossible, Colter turned the head of the canoe to the shore. At the moment of its touching, an Indian seized the rifle belonging to Potts. But Colter, who is a remarkably strong man, immediately retook it. He handed it to Potts, who remained in the canoe, and on receiving it pushed off into the river.

He had scarcely quitted the shore when an arrow was shot at him, and he cried out, "Colter, I am wounded." Colter remonstrated with him on the folly of attempting to escape, and urged him to come ashore.

Instead of complying, he instantly leveled his rifle at an Indian, and shot him dead on the spot. This conduct may appear to have been an act of madness, but it was doubtless the effect of sudden and sound reasoning: If they had taken Potts alive, he must have expected to be tortured to death, according to their custom. He was instantly pierced with arrows so numerous that, to use the language of Colter, "he was made a riddle of."

They now seized Colter, stripped him entirely naked, and began to consult on the manner in which he should be put to death. They were first inclined to set him up as a mark to shoot at. But the chief interfered, and seizing him by the shoulder, asked him if he could run fast.

Colter, who had been some time amongst the Crow Indians, had in a considerable degree acquired the Blackfoot language. He was also well acquainted with Indian customs. He knew that he had now to run for his life, with the dreadful odds of five or six hundred against him. Therefore he cunningly replied that he was a very bad runner—although he was considered by the hunters as remarkably swift.

The chief now commanded the party to remain stationary, and led Colter out on the prairie three or four hundred yards—and released him, bidding him to save himself if he could.

At that instant the horrid war whoop sounded in the ears of poor Colter. Urged with the hope of preserving his life, he ran with a speed at which he was himself surprised.

He proceeded towards the Jefferson's Fork, having to traverse a plain six miles in breadth, abounding with prickly pear, on which he was every instant treading with his naked feet. He ran nearly halfway across the plain before he ventured to look over his shoulder.

He perceived that the Indians were very much scattered—and that he had gained ground to a considerable distance from the main body. But one Indian, who carried a spear, was much before all the rest, and not more than a hundred yards from him.

A faint gleam of hope now cheered the heart of Colter. He derived confidence from the belief that escape was within the bounds of possibility. But that confidence was nearly fatal to him. He had exerted himself to such a degree that the blood gushed from his nostrils—and almost covered the forepart of his body.

He had now arrived within a mile of the river, when he distinctly heard the appalling sound of footsteps behind him, and every instant expected to feel the spear of his pursuer. Again he turned his head, and saw the savage not twenty yards from him.

Determined if possible to avoid the expected blow, he suddenly stopped, turned round, and spread out his arms. The Indian, surprised by the suddenness of the action, and perhaps of the bloody appearance of Colter, also attempted to stop. But exhausted with running, he fell whilst endeavoring to throw his spear, which stuck in the ground and broke in his hand.

Colter instantly snatched up the pointed part, with which he pinned him to the earth, and then continued his flight. The foremost of the Indians, on arriving at the place, stopped till others came up to join them, when they set up a hideous yell. Every moment of this time was improved by Colter, who, although fainting and exhausted, succeeded in gaining the skirting of the cottonwood trees, on the borders of the fork, through which he ran and plunged into the river.

Fortunately for him, a little below this place there was an island, against the upper point of which a raft of drift timber had lodged. He dived under the raft, and after several efforts, got his head above the water amongst the trunks of trees, covered over with smaller wood to the depth of several feet. Scarcely had he secured himself when the Indians arrived on the river, screeching and yelling, as Colter expressed it, "like so many devils." They were frequently on the raft during the day, and were seen through the chinks by Colter, who was congratulating himself on his escape, until the idea arose that they might set the raft on fire.

In horrible suspense he remained until night, when hearing no more of the Indians, he dived under the raft, and swam silently down the river to a considerable distance. He landed and traveled all night. Although happy in having escaped from the Indians, his situation was still dreadful. He was completely naked, under a burning sun—the soles of his feet were entirely filled with the thorns of the prickly pear—and he was hungry. He had no means of killing game—although he saw abundance around him. He was at least seven days' journey from the nearest fort.

These were circumstances under which almost any man but an American hunter would have despaired. He arrived at the fort in seven days, having subsisted on a root much esteemed by the Indians.

— Story adapted from John Bradbury, *Travels in the Interior of America* (London: Sherwood, Neely, and Jones, 1819). Quoted in Charles Griffin Coutant, "The Famous John Colter," *The History of Wyoming from the Earliest Known Discoveries* (Laramie, Wyoming: Chaplin Spafford & Mathison Printers, 1899), 61–69.

The First Written Description of Yellowstone Geysers

(1827)—Daniel T. Potts

A trapper describes geysers, hot springs and a harrowing escape from Indians in a letter to his brother.

Evidence of early mountain man activity is sketchy, but we know that trapper brigades reached the Yellowstone Plateau by 1826. An anonymous account of a trapper's adventures in what is now Yellowstone National Park was published in the Philadelphia Gazette *and* Advertiser *on September 27, 1827.*

The identity of the author was finally revealed in 1947 when two elderly ladies offered to sell the National Park Service three letters that were in their family papers. A fur trapper named Daniel T. Potts had sent one of the letters to his brother on July 8, 1827. It is thought to be the first written description of the thermal features of the upper Yellowstone by someone who actually saw them.

Potts wrote the letter at what is now called Bear Lake in northern Utah. It was then called "Sweet Lake" to distinguish it from Great Salt Lake. Here's Daniel T. Potts's famous "Letter from Sweet Lake."

Sweet Lake
July 8th 1827

Respected Brother,

Shortly after writing to you last year I took my departure for the Black-foot Country. We took a northerly direction about fifty miles where we cross Snake River or the South fork of Columbia—which heads on the top of the great chain of Rocky Mountains that separate the water of the Atlantic from that of the Pacific. Near this place Yellowstone South fork of Missouri and the Henrys fork head at an angular point. The head of the Yellowstone has a large fresh water lake on the very top of the mountain which is as clear as crystal.

On the south borders of this lake is a number of hot and boiling springs—some of water and others of most beautiful fine clay. The springs throw particles to the immense height of from twenty to thirty feet in height. The clay is white and of a pink. The water appears fathomless; it appears to be entirely hollow underneath.

There is also a number of places where the pure sulphur is sent forth in abundance. One of our men visited one of those whilst taking his recreation. There at an instant the earth began a tremendous trembling. With difficulty he made his escape when an explosion took place resembling that of thunder. During our stay in that quarter, I heard it every day.

From this place by a circuitous route to the northwest, we returned. Two others and myself pushed on in the advance for the purpose of accumulating a few more beaver. In the act of passing through a narrow confine in the mountain, we were met plumb in face by a large party of Blackfeet Indians. Not knowing our number, they fled into the mountain in confusion—and we to a small grove of willows. Here we made every preparation for battle. After finding our enemy as much alarmed as ourselves we mounted our horses which were heavily loaded, we took the back retreat.

The Indian raised a tremendous yell and showered down from the mountaintop. They had almost cut off our retreat when we put whip to our horses. They pursued us in close quarters until we reached the plains where we left them behind.

Tomorrow I depart for the west. We are all in good health and hope that this letter will find you in the same situation. I wish you to remember my best respects to all enquiring friends particularly your wife.

Remain yours most affectionately.

Daniel T. Potts

— Adapted from Daniel T. Potts's letter in Aubrey L. Haines, *The Yellowstone Story*, Volume 1 (second ed.) (Boulder: University Press of Colorado, 1977), 41–42.

A Fur Trader Travels to Geyserland

(1834)—W. A. Ferris

A clerk for the American Fur Trading Company hears strange stories at a trappers' rendezvous and goes to see geysers for himself.

Only a few of the rugged mountain men who penetrated the area that became Yellowstone National Park could read and write. One who could was Warren Angus Ferris, a clerk for the American Fur Company.

At the mountain man rendezvous near the present-day Daniel, Wyoming, trappers told Ferris about geothermal features they had seen northwest of there. Ferris was intrigued and decided to see them for himself. That made him Yellowstone's first known tourist, in that his visit was motivated by curiosity instead of commerce.

Ferris kept a journal that was published in serialized form in 1843–1844 in a magazine and later as a book entitled Life in the Rocky Mountains. *In these writings he offered the earliest written descriptions of the Upper Geyser Basin.*

I had heard in the summer of 1833, while at rendezvous, that remarkable boiling springs had been discovered, on the sources of the Madison, by a party of trappers in their spring hunt; of which the accounts they gave, were so very astonishing, that I determined to examine them myself, before recording their descriptions, though I had the united testimony of more than twenty men on the subject, who all declared they saw them, and that they really were, as extensive and remarkable as they had been described.

Having now an opportunity of paying them a visit, and as another or a better might not soon occur, I parted with the company after supper, and, taking with me two Indians, set out at a round pace, the night being clear and comfortable. We proceeded over the plain about twenty miles, and halted until daylight on a fine spring, flowing into Camas Creek.

Refreshed by a few hours' sleep, we started again after a hasty breakfast, and entered a very extensive forest called the Piny Woods, which we passed through, and reached the vicinity of the springs about dark, having seen several small lakes or ponds, on the sources of the Madison; and rode about forty miles; which was a hard day's ride, taking into consideration the rough irregularity of the country through which we had travelled.

We regaled ourselves with a cup of coffee, and immediately after supper lay down to rest, sleepy, and much fatigued. The continual roaring of the springs, however, for some time prevented my going to sleep, and excited an impatient curiosity to examine them; which I was obliged to defer the gratification of, until morning; and filled my slumbers with visions of water spouts, cataracts, fountains, jets d'eau of immense dimensions, etc., etc.

When I arose in the morning, clouds of vapor seemed like a dense fog to overhang the springs, from which frequent reports or explosions of different loudness, constantly assailed our ears. I immediately proceeded to inspect them, and might have exclaimed with the Queen of Sheba, when their full reality of dimensions and novelty burst upon my view, "The half was not told me."

From the surface of a rocky plain or table, burst forth columns of water, of various dimensions, projected high in the air, accompanied by loud explosions, and sulphurous vapors, which were highly disagreeable to the smell. The rock from which these springs burst forth, was calcareous, and probably extends some distance from them, beneath the soil. The largest of these wonderful fountains, projects a column of boiling water several feet in diameter, to the height of more than 150 feet—in my opinion; but the party of Alvarez, who discovered it, persist in declaring that it could not be less than four times that distance in height accompanied with a tremendous noise.

These explosions and discharges occur at intervals of about two hours. After having witnessed three of them, I ventured near enough to put my hand into the water of its basin, but withdrew it instantly, for the heat of the water in this immense cauldron, was altogether too great for comfort, and the agitation of the water, the disagreeable effluvium continually exuding, and the hollow unearthly rumbling under the rock on which I stood, so ill accorded with my notions of personal safety, that I retreated back precipitately to a respectful distance.

The Indians who were with me, were quite appalled, and could not by any means be induced to approach them. They seemed astonished at my presumption in advancing up to the large one, and when I safely returned, congratulated me on my "narrow escape." They believed them to be supernatural, and supposed them to be the production of the Evil Spirit. One of them remarked that hell, of which he had heard from the whites, must be in that vicinity.

The diameter of the basin into which the water of the largest jet principally falls, and from the center of which, through a hole in the rock of about nine or ten feet in diameter, the water spouts up as above related, may be about thirty feet. There are many other smaller fountains, that did not throw their waters up so high, but occurred at shorter intervals. In some instances, the volumes were projected obliquely upwards, and fell into the neighboring fountains or on the rock or prairie. But their ascent was generally perpendicular, falling in and about their own basins or apertures.

These wonderful productions of nature, are situated near the center of a small valley, surrounded by pine covered hills, through which a small fork of the Madison flows. Highly gratified with my visit to these formidable and magnificent fountains, jets, or springs, whichever the reader may please to call them, I set out after dinner to rejoin my companions.

— Quoted from P. Koch, "Discovery of Yellowstone National Park. A Chapter of Early Exploration in the Rocky Mountains," *Magazine of American History with Notes and Queries,* Illustrated, 11, no. 6 (June 1884): 497–505.

Mountain men who trapped in the upper Yellowstone in the early 1800s had never heard the word "geyser" and certainly never expected to see fountains of boiling water shooting into the sky. GALLATIN HISTORY MUSEUM

A Bedtime Story

(c. 1836)—Osborne Russell

A mountain man describes his companions telling tall tales around a campfire in "the infernal regions."

The trappers who visited the Yellowstone Plateau in the early 1800s told about the wonders they had seen, but their reports often were dismissed as tall tales. Perhaps that's because mountain men had a well-developed tradition of entertaining each other by spinning preposterous yarns about their adventures and things they had seen.

Osborne Russell was one of few mountain men who left credible records of their activities. Russell's career as a trapper wasn't remarkable in the sense that he made major discoveries or had grand adventures, but he left his mark on history through a detailed and brightly written account that described the daily activities of the mountain men.

Russell, who visited the upper Yellowstone in the 1830s, described a storytelling session in his famous Journal of a Trapper.

We killed a fat elk and camped at sunset in a smooth, grassy spot between two high, shaggy ridges, watered by a small stream which came tumbling down the gorge behind us.

As we had passed the infernal regions we thought, as a matter of course, this must be a commencement of the Elysian Fields, and accordingly commenced preparing a feast. A large fire was soon blazing, encircled with sides of elk ribs and meat cut in slices, supported on sticks, down which the grease ran in torrents.

The repast being over, the jovial tale goes round the circle, the peals of loud laughter break upon the stillness of the night which, after being mimicked in the echo from rock to rock dies away in the solitary gloom. Every tale reminds an auditor of something similar to it but under different circumstances, which, being told, the "laughing part" gives rise to increasing merriment and furnishes more subjects for good jokes and witty sayings such as a Swift never dreamed of.

Thus the evening passed, with eating, drinking, and stories, enlivened with witty humor until near midnight, all being wrapped in their blankets lying round the fire, gradually falling to sleep one by one, until the last tale is encored by the snoring of the drowsy audience. The speaker takes the hint, breaks off the subject and wrapping his blanket more closely about him, soon joins the snoring party.

The light of the fire being superseded by that of the moon just rising from behind the eastern mountain, a sullen gloom is cast over the remaining fragments of the feast and all is silent except the occasional howling of the solitary wolf on the neighboring mountain, whose senses are attracted by the flavor of roasted meat, but fearing to approach nearer, he sits upon a rock and bewails his calamities in piteous moans which are reechoed among the mountains.

— From Osborne Russell, *Journal of a Trapper or—Nine Years in the Rocky Mountains 1834–1843* (Boise, Idaho: Syms-York, 1921), 49–50.

Jim Bridger's Descriptions
of Yellowstone Wonders

(1852)—John W. Gunnison

An army surveyor attests to the veracity of Jim Bridger's descriptions of Yellowstone's wonders.

Nobody's life story is more entangled in the history of Yellowstone Park than Jim Bridger's. Bridger was only eighteen years old when he came to the Rocky Mountain West in 1822, and he lived there nearly fifty years.

Bridger first visited the upper Yellowstone in 1829 and continued going there into the 1860s. When the bottom fell out of the market for beaver pelts in the 1840s, he established Fort Bridger in northeast Utah to trade with travelers headed west on the Oregon Trail.

Because of his detailed knowledge of native peoples and the geography of the West, the army frequently hired Bridger as a scout and guide. In the spring of 1860, he guided the Raynolds Expedition, which explored the lower Yellowstone Valley but failed to penetrate the area that became Yellowstone National Park because of deep snows.

Bridger developed a reputation as a teller of tall tales, and a number of colorful stories are attributed to him. Conventional wisdom is that people just didn't believe trappers' tales of fountains of boiling water, mountains of glass, and the other wonders of the upper Yellowstone. The US Army apparently found Bridger reliable; they frequently hired him as a scout, included his descriptions in their reports, and called him "Major."

John W. Gunnison, a lieutenant in the Army Corps of Topographers, was one of the officers who believed Bridger. Gunnison was a highly respected Army officer and explorer who lent his name to several cities and natural features in Utah and Colorado.

When a severe winter kept Gunnison from doing surveys of the Great Salt Lake Valley in 1849–1850, he used the time to do research on the people who lived there. He published a book in 1852 that included this description of Bridger.

The builder of Fort Bridger is one of the hardy race of mountain trappers who are now disappearing from the continent, being enclosed in the wave of civilization. These trappers have made a thousand fortunes for eastern men, and by their improvidence have nothing for themselves.

Major Bridger, or "Old Jim," has been more wise of late, and laid aside a competence; but the mountain tastes fostered by twenty-eight years of exciting scenes, will probably keep him there for life. He has been very active, and traversed the region from the headwaters of the Missouri to the Del Norte—and along the Gila to the Gulf, and thence throughout Oregon and the interior of California.

His graphic sketches are delightful romances. With a buffalo-skin and piece of charcoal, he will map out any portion of this immense region, and delineate mountains, streams, and the circular valleys called "holes," with wonderful accuracy; at least we may so speak of that portion we traversed after his descriptions were given.

He gives a picture, most romantic and enticing, of the headwaters of the Yellowstone. A lake twenty miles long, cold and pellucid, lies embosomed amid high precipitous mountains. On the west side is a sloping plain several miles wide, with clumps of trees and groves of pine.

The ground resounds to the tread of horses. Geysers spout up seventy feet high, with a terrific hissing noise, at regular intervals. Waterfalls are sparkling, leaping, and thundering down the precipices, and collect in the pool below. The river issues from this lake, and for fifteen miles roars through the perpendicular canyon at the outlet. In this section are the Great-Springs, so hot that meat is readily cooked in them, and as they descend on the successive terraces, afford at length delightful baths. On the other side is an acid spring, which gushes out in a river torrent; and below is a cave which supplies "vermilion" for the savages in abundance.

Bear, elk, deer, wolf, and fox, are among the sporting game, and the feathered tribe yields its share for variety, on the sportsman's table of rock or turf.

— From J. W. Gunnison, *The Mormons, or, Latter-day Saints: in the Valley of the Great Salt Lake: A History of Their Rise and Progress, Peculiar Doctrines, Present Condition and Prospects; Derived from Personal Observation, During a Residence Among Them* (Philadelphia: Lippincott, Grambo & Co., 1852), 151.

Mountain Men Led a Delicious Life

(1874)—The Earl of Dunraven

Mountain men subsisted in comfort after the fur trade fizzled.

Beginning in 1807, when John Colter first passed through the area that became Yellowstone National Park, through the 1830s, mountain men flourished in the Rocky Mountain West. Then a combination of overtrapping and a shift in men's fashions to silk hats ended the lucrative beaver trade in the 1840s. Although a trapper couldn't earn a fortune after that, a few hardy souls remained in the area and made a subsistence living. Yellowstone tourists encountered such men until the 1880s. Here's a description of an encounter with two mountain men and their entourage written by the Earl of Dunraven, a wealthy Irish nobleman who visited the park in 1874.

In the afternoon we passed quite a patriarchal camp, composed of two men with their Indian wives and several children; half a dozen powerful savage-looking dogs and about fifty horses completed the party.

They had been grazing their stock, hunting, and trapping—leading a nomad, vagabond, and delicious life—a sort of mixed existence, half hunter, half herdsman, and had collected a great pile of deer-hides and beaver-skins. They were then on their way to settlements to dispose of their peltry, and to get stores and provisions; for they were proceeding to look for comfortable winter quarters, down the river or up the canyon.

We soon discovered that the strangers were white, and, moreover, that there were only two men in camp; and without more ado we rode in and made friends. What a lot of mutually interesting information was given and received! We were outward bound and had the news, and the latitude and the longitude. They were homeward bound, had been wandering for months, cut off from all means of communication with the outside world, and had but the vaguest notion of their position on the globe.

But, though ignorant of external matters and what was going on in settlements, they had not lost all desire for information. An American, although he lives with an Indian woman in the forests or on the plains, never quite loses his interest in politics and parties; and these two squaw-men were very anxious to hear all about electioneering matters.

These men looked very happy and comfortable. Unquestionably the proper way for a man to travel with ease and luxury in these deserts is for him to take unto himself a helpmate chosen from the native population. With an Indian wife to look after his bodily comforts, a man may devote himself to hunting, fishing, or trapping without a thought or care. He may make his mind quite easy about all household matters. His camp will be well arranged, the tent pegs driven securely home, the stock watered, picketed, and properly cared for, a good supper cooked, his bed spread out, and everything made comfortable; his clothes and hunting-gear looked after, the buttons sewn on his shirt (if he has got any shirt—or any buttons) and all the little trivial incidents of life, which, if neglected, wear out one's existence, he will find carefully attended to by a willing and affectionate slave.

They had a lot to tell us also about their travels and adventures, about the wood and water supply, and the abundance or deficiency of game. So we sat down on bales of beaver-skins and retailed all the civilized intelligence we could think of. The women came and brought us embers for our pipes, and spread out robes for us and made us at home. And the little, fat, chubby children, wild and shy as young wolves, peered at us from behind the tent out of their round, black, beady eyes.

— The Earl of Dunraven, *The Great Divide: Travels in the Upper Yellowstone in the Summer of 1874* (London: Chatto and Windus Piccadilly, 1876), 209–212.

PART 2:
PROSPECTORS AND EXPLORERS

INTRODUCTION

Intrepid men scour the upper Yellowstone for gold and fame.

In the mid 1800s, the US government sent topographers to map the West, inventory resources, and find routes for railroads. The remote area that would become Yellowstone National Park was the last major area in the country to be explored. Even the foreboding Grand Canyon of the Colorado River was mapped before government explorers ventured onto the Yellowstone Plateau.

In 1859 the army ordered Colonel William F. Raynolds to explore the Yellowstone River, but deep snow prevented him from entering the area that became Yellowstone National Park. Based on conversations with his guide, mountain man Jim Bridger, Raynolds included descriptions of Yellowstone geysers in his official report, but that wasn't published until 1868.

The Civil War curtailed army explorations, leaving the upper Yellowstone terra incognita. Then gold was discovered in Montana in the 1860s, and prospectors began scouring every gulch and gully, including the area that became Yellowstone Park.

At first, accounts of wonders at the heads of the Yellowstone and Madison rivers were dismissed as tall tales. But as the reports accumulated, it became apparent that there really were things to see—a crystal-clear sea perched on the top of the mountains, a canyon a thousand feet deep, petrified forests, and fountains that sent boiling water up hundreds of feet.

In the late 1860s several efforts to launch expeditions to explore the upper Yellowstone fizzled, because organizers could not recruit enough men to repel Indian attacks. Then in 1869 three men figured Indians wouldn't notice a small group and successfully explored the area, but reports of the Folsom-Cook-Peterson expedition didn't garner much attention. The next year a group of prominent Montana officials and businessmen had more success. That was the famous Washburn Expedition, whose adventures are chronicled in part 3 of this book.

Reports from the Washburn Expedition of 1870 stimulated so much interest in the upper Yellowstone that the US government decided to send two expeditions to systematically explore the area the next year. One was under the direction of Dr. Ferdinand V. Hayden of the US Geological Survey, and another was under Colonel John W. Barlow of the Army Corps of Engineers. The two expeditions worked in tandem to measure and map the wonders of the area. The reports of these expeditions helped persuade Congress to create Yellowstone National Park—the first national park in the world.

Snow Prevents Army from Exploring Wonderland

(1860)—W. F. Raynolds

An army mapmaker fails to penetrate the upper Yellowstone, even with Jim Bridger's help.

In 1859 the army ordered Colonel William F. Raynolds to explore the course of the Yellowstone River from its mouth in western North Dakota to its source in northwest Wyoming. Raynolds successfully mapped the lower Yellowstone, but when he reached the edge of the area that was to be Yellowstone Park in 1860, snow prevented him from entering.

The famous mountain man Jim Bridger served as Raynold's guide, and the colonel quoted his description of geysers in an official report. Here's an excerpt from Raynolds's report.

West of the Big Horn, the other tributaries of the Yellowstone are Pryor's river, Clark's fork, the Big Rosebud, and Beaver River. These streams are comparatively short and small, find their sources in the mountains, and flow to the north.

Beyond these is the valley of the Upper Yellowstone, which is, as yet, a terra incognita. My expedition passed entirely around, but could not penetrate it. My intention was to enter it from the head of Wind River, but the basaltic ridge previously spoken of intercepted our route and prohibited the attempt.

After this obstacle had thus forced us over on the western slope of the Rocky Mountains, an effort was made to recross and reach the district in question; but, although it was June, the immense body of snow baffled all our exertions, and we were compelled to content ourselves with listening to marvellous tales of burning plains, immense lakes, and boiling springs, without being able to verify these wonders.

I know of but two white men who claim to have ever visited this part of the Yellowstone Valley—James Bridger and Robert Meldrum. The narratives of both these men are very remarkable, and Bridger, in one of his recitals, described an immense boiling spring that is a perfect counterpart of the geysers of Iceland. As he is uneducated, and had probably never heard of the existence of such natural marvels elsewhere, I have little doubt that he spoke of that which he had actually seen.

The burning plains described by these men may be volcanic, or more probably burning beds of lignite, similar to those on Powder River, which are known to be in a state of ignition. Bridger also insisted that immediately west of the point at which we made our final effort to penetrate this singular valley, there is a stream of considerable size, which divides and flows down either side of the watershed, thus discharging its waters into both the Atlantic and Pacific oceans. Having seen this phenomenon on a small scale in the highlands of Maine, where a rivulet discharges a portion of its waters into the Atlantic and the remainder into the St. Lawrence, I am prepared to concede that Bridger's "Two Ocean River" may be a verity.

Had our attempt to enter this district been made a month later in the season, the snow would have mainly disappeared, and there would have been no insurmountable obstacles to overcome. I cannot doubt, therefore, that at no very distant day the mysteries of this region will be fully revealed, and though small in extent, I regard the valley of the upper Yellowstone as the most interesting unexplored district in our widely expanded country.

— Excerpt from Report of Brevet Colonel W. F. Raynolds, "U.S. Army Corps of Engineers on the Explorations of the Yellowstone and Missouri Rivers in 1859–60" (Washington, DC: Government Printing Office, 1868), 10-11.

An Optimistic Prospector

(1863)—Walter DeLacy

Prospectors, sure they'll hit pay dirt, decide on the rules for staking gold claims.

In 1863 Walter Washington DeLacy led a forty-man expedition that explored the Snake River to its source inside the area that became Yellowstone National Park. The party didn't find enough "color" (gold) for a paying proposition, but they did bring back a wealth of information about the Yellowstone Plateau.

DeLacy included that information in his famous 1865 map of the Montana territory. If he had published an account of his trip in the 1860s, DeLacy probably would be remembered as the "discoverer of Yellowstone Park," but it was more than thirty years before he did that.

At a time when a man could make a fortune from a few gold pans of dirt, prospectors were ever hopeful of striking it rich. In the virtually lawless territories, prospecting parties made their own rules to assure that everybody had a fair chance. Here's DeLacy's description of an effort to draft some "miners' laws."

I halted the men at the creek as they came up, and when all had arrived I suggested to them that we should go on to the next water, pick out a good camp, and remain some days and prospect the different streams, which were in sight. This was agreed to, and we went forward about three miles to the next creek, near the outlet of Lake Jackson and established ourselves where wood, water, and grass were abundant.

After unpacking and staking the animals out, another meeting was called in order to decide upon our future action. It was decided to build a "corral," to put the horses in at night that should be left in camp, and that four parties should be formed: one to remain in camp as a guard, and three others to prospect the streams in sight.

The men were then detailed for the different expeditions, and it was suggested, that as there was a strong probability of finding good "diggings," we should adopt some mining laws for them.

We therefore organized ourselves into a "miners' meeting," and, after appointing a chairman, etc., one of the members moved, and another seconded the motion, that the following regulations should be adopted:

1. That every person present should be regarded as a discoverer in each and every gulch found by any party or member of a party.

2. That each member, as discoverer, should be entitled to five claims of two hundred feet each along the gulch, viz., a discovery claim, and a preemption claim in the main gulch, a bar claim, a hill claim, and a patch claim. (I never knew exactly what a patch claim was, but I think that it meant all that you could grab, after you got the other four claims.)

These liberal and disinterested regulations were voted in the affirmative with gratifying unanimity, and the chairman was just about to put the question to the meeting whether there was any more business before it, when a big, burly Scotchman named Brown, who had apparently been turning the subject over in his mind, jumped up, and inquired with great earnestness, "But, Mr. Chairman, what shall we do with the rest of it."

— Excerpt adapted from Walter W. DeLacy, "A Trip Up the South Snake River in 1863," *Contributions to the Historical Society of Montana 2* (1896): 113–143.

Documenting Prospector Tales of Boiling Fountains

(1869)—Charles W. Cook and David E. Folsom

Three brave men sneak past hostile Indians to see Yellowstone's wonders for themselves.

By the late 1860s enough prospectors' reports of boiling fountains, deep canyons, and glass mountains had accumulated to convince people that there were things worth seeing on the upper Yellowstone. Several plans for expeditions to document the wonders of the area fizzled because organizers couldn't recruit large enough groups to feel safe from Indians. But in 1869 David Folsom, Charles Cook, and William Peterson decided that a small group could avoid the hostiles.

These intrepid explorers succeeded in finding the canyons, falls, and geysers, but publishers were leery of their stories. Both the New York Tribune *and* Scribner's *magazine refused to publish an account of the Cook–Folsom–Peterson expedition, because "they had reputation that could not risk such unreliable material." A Chicago-based magazine,* Western Monthly, *finally published it in July 1870, nearly a year after the trip. The* Monthly *attributed the story to C. W. Cook.*

The account didn't get wide circulation until nearly thirty-five years later, when it was published by the Montana Historical Society. Nathaniel Pitt Langford, who wrote a preface for the historical society version, attributed it to David E. Folsom. Here's the Cook/Folsom description of geysers and hot springs.

We ascended to the head of the lake and remained in its vicinity for several days, resting ourselves and our horses and viewing the many objects of interest and wonder. Among these were springs differing from any we had previously seen. They were situated along the shore for a distance of two miles, extending back from it about five hundred yards and into the lake perhaps as many feet. The ground in many places gradually sloped down to the water's edge, while in others the white chalky cliffs rose fifteen feet high, the waves having worn the rock away at the base, leaving the upper portion projecting over in some places twenty feet.

There were several hundred springs here, varying in size from miniature fountains to pools or wells seventy-five feet in diameter and of great depth. The water had a pale violet tinge and was very clear, enabling us to discern small objects fifty or sixty feet below the surface. In some of these, vast openings led off at the side, and as the slanting rays of the sun lit up these deep caverns, we could see the rocks hanging from their roofs, their water-worn sides and rocky floors, almost as plainly as if we had been traversing their silent chambers.

These springs were intermittent, flowing or boiling at irregular intervals. The greater portion of them were perfectly quiet while we were there, although nearly all gave unmistakable evidence of frequent activity. Some of them would quietly settle for ten feet, while another would as quietly rise until it overflowed its banks, and send a torrent of hot water sweeping down to the lake. At the same time, one near at hand would send up a sparkling jet of water ten or twelve feet high, which would fall back into its basin, and then perhaps instantly stop boiling and quietly settle into the earth, or suddenly rise and discharge its waters in every direction over the rim; while another, as if wishing to attract our wondering gaze, would throw up a cone six feet in diameter and eight feet high, with a loud roar.

These changes, each one of which would possess some new feature, were constantly going on; sometimes they would occur within the space of a few minutes, and again hours would elapse before any change could be noted. At the water's edge, along the lake shore, there were several mounds of solid stone, on the top of each of which was a small basin with a perforated bottom. These also overflowed at times, and the hot water trickled down on every side. Thus, by the slow process of precipitation, through the countless lapse of ages, these stone monuments have been formed. A small cluster of mud springs nearby claimed our attention. They were like hollow truncated cones and oblong mounds, three or four feet in height. These were filled with mud, resembling thick paint of the finest quality, differing in color from pure white to the various shades of yellow, pink, red, and violet. Some of these boiling pots were less than a foot in diameter. The mud in them would slowly rise and fall, as the bubbles of escaping steam, following one after the other, would burst upon the surface. During the afternoon they threw mud to the height of fifteen feet for a few minutes, and then settled back to their former quietude.

As we were about departing on our homeward trip, we ascended the summit of a neighboring hill and took a final look at Yellowstone Lake. Nestled among the forest crowned hills which bounded our vision, lay this inland sea, its crystal waves dancing and sparkling in the sunlight as if laughing with joy for their wild freedom. It is a scene of transcendent beauty which has been viewed by but few white men, and we felt glad to have looked upon it before its primeval solitude should be broken by the crowds of pleasure seekers which at no distant day will throng its shores.

September 29th, we took up our march for home. Our plan was to cross the range in a northwesterly direction, find the Madison River, and follow it down to civilization. Twelve miles brought us to a small triangular-shaped lake, about eight miles long, deeply set among the hills. We kept on in a northwesterly direction as near as the rugged nature of the country would permit, and on the third day came to a small irregularly shaped valley, some six miles across in the widest place, from every part of which great clouds of steam arose. From descriptions which we had had of this valley from persons who had previously visited it, we recognized it as the place known as "Burnt Hole" or "Death Valley." The Madison River flows through it, and from the general contour of the country we knew that it headed in the lake: which we passed two days ago, only twelve miles from the Yellowstone. We descended into the valley and found that the springs had the same general characteristics as those I have already described, although some of them were much larger and discharged a vast amount of water. One of them, at a little distance, attracted our attention by the immense amount of steam it threw off, and upon approaching it we found it to be an intermittent geyser in active operation. The hole through which the water was discharged was ten feet in diameter, and was situated in the center of a large circular shallow basin, into which the water fell. There was a stiff breeze blowing at the time, and by going to the windward side and carefully picking our way over convenient stones, we were enabled to reach the edge of the hole. At that moment the escaping steam was causing the water to boil up in a fountain five or six feet high. It stopped in an instant, and commenced settling down—twenty, thirty, forty feet—until we concluded that the bottom had fallen out, but the next instant, without any warning, it came rushing up and shot into the air at least eighty feet, causing us to stampede for higher ground. It continued to spout at intervals of a few minutes for some time, but finally subsided and was quiet during the remainder of the time we stayed in the vicinity.

We followed up the Madison five miles, and there found the most gigantic hot springs we had seen. They were situated along the river bank, and discharged so much hot water that the river was blood warm a quarter of a mile below. One of the springs was 250 feet in diameter, and had every indication of spouting powerfully at times. The waters from the hot springs in this valley, if united, would form a large stream, and they increase the size of the river nearly one half. Although we experienced no bad effects from passing through the "Valley of Death," yet we were not disposed to dispute the propriety of giving it that name. It seemed to be shunned by all animated nature. There were no fish in the river, no birds in the trees, no animals—not even a track—anywhere to be seen, although in one spring we saw the entire skeleton of a buffalo that had probably fallen in accidentally and been boiled down to soup.

Leaving this remarkable valley, we followed the course of the Madison, sometimes through level valleys, and sometimes through deep cuts in mountain ranges, and on the fourth of October emerged from a canyon, ten miles long with high and precipitous mountain sides, to find the broad valley of the Lower Madison spread out before us. Here we could recognize familiar landmarks in some of the mountain peaks around Virginia City. From this point we completed our journey by easy stages, and arrived at home on the evening of the eleventh. We had been absent thirty-six days—a much longer time than our friends had anticipated and we found that they were seriously contemplating organizing a party to go in search of us.

— Excerpt from David E. Folsom, "The Valley of the Upper Yellowstone," *Contributions to the Historical Society of Montana* 5 (1904): 365–369.

Finding a Goldilocks Pool at Mammoth Hot Springs

(1871)—John W. Barlow

Soldier-explorers sample hot springs pools to find the perfect temperature for a bath.

Reports from the Washburn Expedition of 1870 stimulated so much interest in the upper Yellowstone that the US government decided to send two expeditions to systematically explore the area the next year. One was under the direction of Dr. Ferdinand V. Hayden of the US Geological Survey, and another was under Colonel John W. Barlow of the Army Corps of Engineers. The two expeditions worked in tandem to measure and map the wonders of the area. One of those wonders was "Soda Mountain," which is now known as Mammoth Hot Springs.

In an era when water for bathing often was heated in a teakettle, the copious amount of hot water flowing down the mountainside at Mammoth Hot Springs intrigued the explorers. Here's how Colonel Barlow described it.

A system of hot springs of great beauty, flowing from the top and sides of a large hill of calcareous deposit, and called Soda Mountain, is found five miles up the left bank of Gardner's River. Here, at the foot of this curious white mountain, we encamped, and remained until the 24th [of July], examining the wonderful spring formation of this region, and the country around it.

The central point of interest is the Soda Mountain, occupying an area of a hundred acres, and rising like the successive steps of a cascade, to the height of over 200 feet above the plateau at its base. The upper surface is a plain, composed of many hot springs, constantly sending up volumes of vapor slightly impregnated with sulphurous fumes.

The sides of the hill down which the waters of these hot springs flow have become terraced into steps of various heights and widths, some twelve

Jupiter Terrace at Mammoth Hot Springs enticed bathers with hot water at a variety of temperatures.
WILLIAM HENRY JACKSON, NATIONAL PARK SERVICE

inches in dimension, while others are as many feet. In each terrace there is generally a pool of water, standing in a scalloped basin of gypsum, deposited at the edges by the water as it becomes cooler. These basins are often tinged with pink, gray, and yellow colors, giving to the whole a very beautiful effect.

The rock in all directions has evidently been deposited in the same manner as the Soda Mountain is now being built up. When the formation ceases from a change in the course of the water, the rock becomes friable and disintegrates. After a time, vegetation springs up and covers the surface. Many of the basins have the size and shape of bathtubs, and were used by members of the party for bathing purposes. The temperature varies in the different pools from fifty degrees all the way up to 180, so there is no difficulty in finding a bath of suitable temperature.

[A few days later, Barlow left Mammoth Hot Springs to explore the area. When he returned, he enjoyed the hot water again.]

Toward evening I enjoyed a bath among the natural basins of Soda Mountain. The temperature was delightful, and could be regulated at pleasure by simply stepping from one basin to another. They were even quite luxurious, being lined with spongy gypsum, soft and pleasant to the touch. I walked over a part of the hill by the faint light of the new moon, which gave to its deep-blue pools of steaming water a wild and ghostly appearance. The photographer has taken numerous views of these springs and the country in their vicinity, which will serve to convey a much more definite idea of their beautiful formation than can be given by any written description. A special survey was made of this locality, and careful observations of its latitude and longitude.

— Excerpts from Colonel John W. Barlow, *Report of a Reconnaissance of the Basin of the Upper Yellowstone in 1871*, 42nd Cong., 2nd sess., Senate Ex Doc. 66 (1871): 2–43.

Lord Blackmore Riles His Guide by Catching 254 Fish

(1872)—Jack Bean

An old Indian fighter vents disgust at an English nobleman's profligacy.

In the 1870s a curious conflict developed over who got to kill wildlife in Yellowstone Park. After decimating the bison herds on the Great Plains, hide hunters converged on the park and slaughtered elk by the thousands, leaving their carcasses to rot.

Sport hunters condemned commercial hunting, but reserved their own right to blast away at anything that moved. On the other hand, hide hunters said they were just trying to make a living and condemned killing "just for fun."

The differing attitudes are illustrated in the story below. It comes from the reminiscence of Jack Bean, an Indian fighter and commercial hunter who was hired on as a guide to the Hayden Expedition of 1872.

Lord William Blackmore, a wealthy Englishman who had helped fund the expedition, was Hayden's guest and an avid fisherman. Here's what Bean says happened when he went fishing with Lord Blackmore.

While the doctor was geologizing the country there, I went fishing with Sir William Blackmore in Lake Abundance.

You could see plenty of trout close to shore in the lake, but when he got to catching them he thought it would be wonderful if he caught one for each year he was old—fifty four. He soon caught the fifty four and tried for a hundred, and was not long catching this and made a try for fifty-four more and kept fishing for another hundred, and another fifty-four.

As we had gotten two thirds of the way around the lake by this time, I told him that I would quit as I had all the fish I could drag along on the grass, being 250. I dragged them into camp which was close along the lake and wanted to make a little show of these fish.

Sir Blackmore, whenever he would see any bones would always ask, "How come those bones there?" I would tell him they were left by skin hunters in the winter. He thought that all skin hunters should be put in jail for such vandalism and I told him he would do the same if he were in this country for the winter.

So when I had shook all these fish off from the strings they made such a sight that I called Dr. Hayden's attention to what Sir Blackmore would do if he had a chance. He colored up considerable and excused himself by saying, "It was Godsend to catch some of them out."

— Adapted from Jack Bean, "Real Hunting Tales," Typescript, Gallatin History Museum, 33–34.

Sidford's Fall on Grand Mountain

(1872)—N. P. Langford

A young Englishman nearly loses his life when he tumbles down Grand Teton.

Sidford Hamp was just seventeen in 1872 when his uncle, William Blackmore, fulfilled his dreams by landing him a job on the second Hayden Expedition to Yellowstone Park.

Lord Blackmore was wealthy and well connected, so he was able to arrange for Sidford to dine with dignitaries in Washington, D.C., meet the famous Sioux Chief Red Cloud, visit Niagara Falls, and travel across America on the new transcontinental railroad.

Perhaps Sidford's biggest adventure occurred on July 29, when he accompanied Hayden's second in command, Captain James Stevenson, and Yellowstone National Park's first superintendent, N. P. Langford, as they mounted an effort to climb the 13,775-foot Grand Teton Peak in Wyoming. Some say Langford and Stevenson surmounted a side peak, not the pinnacle of Grand Teton, but it was a grand adventure in any case. Here's Langford's description of what happened to Sidford that day.

Very soon after we commenced the ascent, we found ourselves clambering around projecting ledges of perpendicular rocks, inserting our fingers into crevices so far beyond us that we reached them with difficulty, and poising our weight upon shelves not exceeding two inches in width, jutting from the precipitous walls of gorges from fifty to 300 feet in depth. This toilsome process, which severely tested our nerves, was occasionally interrupted by large banks of snow, which had lodged upon some of the projections or in the concavities of the mountain side—in passing over the yielding surface of which we obtained tolerable foothold, unless, as was often the case, there was a groundwork of ice beneath.

When this occurred, we found the climbing difficult and hazardous. In many places, the water from the melting snow had trickled through it, and congealed the lower surface. This, melting in turn, had worn long openings between the ice and the mountainside, from two to four feet in width, down which we could look 200 feet or more. Great care was necessary to avoid slipping into these crevices. An occasional spur of rock or ice, connecting the ice-wall with the mountain, was all that held these patches of snow in their places. In Europe, they would have been called glaciers.

Distrustful as we all were of their permanency, we were taught, before our toil was ended, to wish there had been more of them. As a general thing, they were more easily surmounted than the bare rock precipices, though on one occasion they came near proving fatal to one of our party.

Mr. Hamp, fresh from his home in England, knew little of the properties of snow and ice, and at one of the critical points in our ascent, trusting too much to their support, slipped and fell. For a moment, his destruction seemed inevitable, but with admirable dexterity, he threw himself astride the icy ridge projecting from the mountain.

Impelled by this movement, with one leg dangling in the crevice next the mountain side, and the other sweeping the snow outside the glacier, he slid with fearful rapidity, at an angle of forty-five degrees, for the distance of fifty feet, falling headlong into a huge pile of soft snow, which prevented his descent of a thousand feet or more down the precipitous side of the mountain.

I saw him fall, and supposed he would be dashed to pieces. A moment afterwards, he crawled from the friendly snow heap and rejoined us unharmed, and we all united in a round of laughter, as thankful as it was hearty.

— Excerpt from N. P. Langford, "The Ascent of Mount Hayden," *Scribner's Monthly* 6, no. 3 (June 1873): 129–157.

PART 3:
THE WASHBURN EXPEDITION

Introduction

Ambitious men seek fame and fortune by documenting the wonders of the upper Yellowstone.

There had been rumors of wonders in the upper Yellowstone for more than fifty years, but the Washburn Expedition of 1870 made it official. The place really did contain towering waterfalls, a huge inland sea, and stupendous boiling fountains that threw water hundreds of feet into the air.

There were several reasons Washburn and his companions captured the public imagination when earlier efforts failed. First, the expedition was composed of prominent government officials and businessmen whose word could not be doubted. Second, the expedition included several skilled writers who published reports immediately after they returned from the wilderness. Third, there was a well-developed communication system that included several Montana territorial newspapers and the telegraph to spread the news across the nation. Finally, the Northern Pacific Railroad, which was making its way westward, promoted the area in hopes of making it a tourist destination.

Just as important as the credibility of members of the Washburn Expedition was their writing skill. Several expedition members wrote articles about the trip for the Helena Herald *that were reprinted around the world. Also, N. P. Langford, Truman Everts, and Walter Trumbull published articles in national magazines.*

Naming Tower Fall

(1870)—N. P. Langford

**_Members of the famous Washburn expedition engineer
a double-cross while naming the sights._**

_Nathaniel Pitt Langford helped organize the Washburn Expedition and was one
of its principal chroniclers. His two-part article in the May and June 1871 issues
of_ Scribner's Monthly _brought national attention to Yellowstone's wonders, and
his 1905 book documented the expedition's activities._

_In 1864 Langford was appointed collector of internal revenue for the new
Montana Territory, a position he held for five years. Then he resigned to accept an
appointment as territorial governor, but the Senate refused to confirm him._

_After his visit to Yellowstone, Langford lectured on the East Coast and worked
to get the area declared a national park. He became the first Yellowstone Park
superintendent, a position he held from 1872 to 1877._

_Explorers on the Washburn Expedition always had to be alert for the dangers
of Indians, wild animals, and strange geothermal features, but they also found
ways to have fun. Here's Langford's description of one of the pranks they played
on each other._

At the outset of our journey we had agreed that we would not give to any
object of interest that we might discover the name of any of our party nor of
our friends. This rule was to be religiously observed.

While in camp on Sunday, August 28th, on the bank of this creek, it
was suggested that we select a name for the creek and fall. Walter Trumbull
suggested "Minaret Creek" and "Minaret Fall." Mr. Hauser suggested "Tower
Creek" and "Tower Fall." After some discussion a vote was taken, and by a
small majority, the name "Minaret" was decided upon.

During the following evening Mr. Hauser stated with great seriousness that we had violated the agreement made relative to naming objects for our friends. He said that the well known Southern family—the Rhetts—lived in St. Louis, and that they had a most charming and accomplished daughter named "Minnie." He said that this daughter was a sweetheart of Trumbull, who had proposed the name—her name—"Minnie Rhett"—and that we had unwittingly given to the fall and creek the name of this sweetheart of Mr. Trumbull.

Mr. Trumbull indignantly denied the truth of Hauser's statement, and Hauser as determinedly insisted that it was the truth. The vote was therefore reconsidered, and by a substantial majority it was decided to substitute the name "Tower" for "Minaret." Later, and when it was too late to recall or reverse the action of our party, it was surmised that Hauser himself had a sweetheart in St. Louis—a Miss Tower.

— Excerpt from N. P. Langford, *Diary of the Washburn Expedition to the Yellowstone and Firehole Rivers* (Saint Paul, MN: Frank J. Haines, Footnote, 1905), 22–23.

To the Bottom of Yellowstone Canyon

(1870)—Gustavus Doane

The leader of the army escort sees daytime stars at the bottom of a sunless canyon.

Lieutenant Gustavus Cheyney Doane wanted to be a famous explorer and lobbied his superiors to be assigned as commander of the army escort for the Washburn Expedition. It worked. His official report circulated widely and helped thrust the wonders of the upper Yellowstone into public view.

Doane developed a reputation as "the man who invented wonderland," and he accompanied the Hayden and Barlow Expeditions to Yellowstone National Park in 1871 and an excursion by Secretary of War William Belknap in 1874. He sought to be named park superintendent in 1889 and 1891, but his aspirations were denied.

Here's Doane's description of going to the bottom of Yellowstone Canyon.

Selecting the channel of a small creek, and leaving the horses, I followed it down on foot, wading in the bed of the stream, which fell off at an angle about 30 degrees, between walls of the gypsum. Private McConnell accompanied me. On entering the ravine, we came at once to hot springs of sulphur, sulphate of copper, alum, steam jets, etcetera, in endless variety, some of them of very peculiar form. One of them in particular, of sulphur, had built up a tall spire from the slope of the wall, standing out like an enormous horn, with hot water trickling down its sides. The creek ran on a bed of solid rock, in many places smooth and slippery, in other obstructed by masses of debris formed from the overhanging cliffs of the sulphurated limestone above.

After descending for three miles in the channel, we came to a sort of bench or terrace, the same one seen previously in following down the creek from our first camp in the basin. Here we found a large flock of mountain sheep, very tame, and greatly astonished, no doubt, at our sudden appearance. McConnell killed one and wounded another, whereupon the rest

Explorers marveled at the sight of the Lower Falls of the Yellowstone and scaled the steep canyon walls. WILLIAM HENRY JACKSON, NATIONAL PARK SERVICE

disappeared, clambering up the steep walls with a celerity truly astonishing. We were now 1,500 feet below the brink. From here the creek channel was more precipitous, and for a mile we climbed downward over masses of rock and fallen trees, splashing in warm water, ducking under cascades, and skirting close against sideling places to keep from falling into boiling caldrons in the channel.

After four hours of hard labor since leaving the horses, we finally reached the bottom of the gulf and the margin of the Yellowstone, famished with thirst, wet and exhausted. The river water here is quite warm and of a villainously alum and sulphurous taste. Its margin is lined with all kinds of chemical springs, some depositing craters of calcareous rock, others muddy, black, blue, slaty, or reddish water. The internal heat renders the atmosphere oppressive, though a strong breeze draws through the canyon. A frying sound comes constantly to the ear, mingled with the rush of the current. The place abounds with sickening and purgatorial smells.

We had come down the ravine at least four miles, and looking upward the fearful wall appeared to reach the sky. It was about 3 o'clock p.m., and stars could be distinctly seen, so much of the sunlight was cut off from entering the chasm. Tall pines on the extreme verge appeared the height of two or three feet. The canyon, as before said, was in two benches, with a plateau on either side, about half way down. This plateau, about a hundred yards in width, looked from below like a mere shelf against the wall; the total depth was not less than 2,500 feet, and more probably 3,000. There are perhaps other canyons longer and deeper than this one, but surely none combining grandeur and immensity with peculiarity of formation and profusion of volcanic or chemical phenomena.

Returning to the summit, we were five hours reaching our horses, by which time darkness had set in, and we were without a trail, in the dense forest, having fallen timber to evade and treacherous marshes to cross on our way to camp. I knew the general direction, however, and took a straight course, using great caution in threading the marshes, wherein our horses sank in up to their bodies nevertheless. Fortune favored us, and we arrived in camp at 11 o'clock at night, wet and chilled to the bone.

— Excerpt adapted from the Report of Lieutenant Gustavus C. Doane Upon the So-Called Yellowstone Expedition of 1870 (Washington, DC: Government Printing Office, 1871), 13–14.

Viewing Yellowstone Lake

(1870)—Walter Trumbull

*A reporter says Yellowstone Lake is like
"the broad hand of an honest German."*

Walter Trumbull was the son of US Senator Lyman Trumbull of Illinois and had been an assistant assessor of internal revenue for Montana Territory before he joined the Washburn Expedition. He was a special correspondent for the Helena Herald *and published an account of his Yellowstone experience in the* Overland Monthly. *Here's his description of Yellowstone Lake.*

After remaining one day in the vicinity of the first geyser, we forded the Yellowstone just above our camp, and shaped our course for the lake. At the ford the river was quite wide, and a narrow bench of rock rose up from the bottom, stretching from bank to bank. On this bench the water was about three feet deep, but on either side of it was a foot or two deeper. In fording the stream, each man led a pack animal. All did very well while they kept upon the bench. Occasionally some one would get into deeper water, and become drenched, but he had the benefit of encouraging cheers from those who had crossed in safety, and who stood ready to welcome him upon the anticipated shore.

From the ford to the lake—a distance of about ten miles—our course was generally through timber, much of which had been blown down by strong winds, rendering traveling exceedingly tedious and difficult. In open places near the river we were continually meeting with mud-springs, some of them of a considerable magnitude.

At one point in the river we discovered a short series of rapids, between high, rocky banks; the one on the east side rising to the proportion of a bluff. After fording a stream, about one-third the size of the Yellowstone, emptying into the lake, we camped on the edge of the timber, about a hundred yards from the lakeshore.

Yellowstone Lake is a lonely, but lovely inland sea, everywhere surrounded by "forests primeval," and nestled in the bosom of the Rocky Mountains. Some trappers have insisted that its waters ran both to the Atlantic and the Pacific, but such is not the case. The summit of the main chain, however, approaches within half a mile of its south shore, and in places the divide is very little above the lake.

Its shape resembles the broad hand of an honest German, who has had his forefinger and the two adjoining shot off at the second joint, while fighting for glory and Emperor William. The palm of the hand represents the main body, or north part, of the lake. The fingers and thumb, spread to their utmost extent—the thumb and little finger being much the longest—represent inlets indenting the south shore, and stretching inland, as if to wash away the Rocky Mountains.

Between these inlets project high, rocky promontories, covered with dense timber. The largest stream flows into the lake at its upper end, or the extreme southeast corner. This stream is really the Yellowstone River, which, for a distance of thirty miles, has an average width of over fifteen miles. This enlargement constitutes the lake, which, after being augmented by several smaller streams, narrows down to the width of an eighth of a mile, and flows northward toward the great falls.

The mood of the lake is ever changing; the character of its shore is ever varying. At one moment, it is placid and glassy as a calm summer's sea; at the next, "it breaks into dimples, and laughs in the sun." Half an hour later, beneath a stormy sky, its waters may be broken and lashed into an angry and dangerous sea, like the short, choppy waves which rise in storms on Lake Erie and Lake Michigan.

Where we first saw it, it had a glittering beach of gray and rock crystal sand, but as we continued around it, we found rocky and muddy shores, gravel beaches—on which several varieties of chalcedony were profusely scattered—and hot springs in abundance. Near the southeast end of the lake is the highest peak in the vicinity. It is steep and barren, and from the lakeshore appears to taper to a point.

On the south side is a precipice, nearly a thousand feet high. Two of the party ascended it. It took them all of one day to make the trip and return. About two-thirds of the way up they were obliged to leave their horses, and continue the ascent on foot. The altitude of the mountain, as obtained by observations with the barometer and thermometer, was 11,163 feet. Much snow was found before reaching the summit.

A fine view of the surrounding country, and a good idea of the shape of the lake, were obtained. Immense steam-jets were seen to the south; but as our time was becoming somewhat limited, we did not remain to visit them. Several barometrical calculations were made; and we determined the height of the lake to be 8,300 feet.

On the south side of the lake we found dense timber, much of which was fallen. Through it were no trails, and traveling was exceedingly difficult. Many large trees had fallen, with their branches clear out into the lake, rendering it very hard to follow the lakeshore. We, however, kept the shore as much as possible, except when we cut across the bases of the promontories; though on one occasion we crossed a low divide in the main chain, and camped on the headwaters of Snake River, without finding it out for a day or two afterward. We thought the brook on which we were camped circled around, and ran into the lake.

— Excerpt from Walter Trumbull, "The Washburn Expedition," *Overland Monthly* 6, no. 6 (June 1871): 489–490.

First Report of Cooking Live Fish in a Hot Spring

(1870)—Cornelius Hedges

An angler accidentally flips a live fish into a boiling spring, discovering a new way to cook.

Many early Yellowstone travelers described places like the Fishing Cone, where anglers could catch a fish in cool water and then cook it in a nearby hot spring without taking it off the hook. In fact, Philetus Norris, the park's second superintendent, used to demonstrate the feat for the amusement of tourists. The earliest written description of cooking live fish in a hot spring was written by Cornelius Hedges, who accidentally discovered the trick while on the Washburn Expedition.

Hedges came to Montana to look for gold, but soon gave that up to set up a law practice in Helena. After returning from the Yellowstone, Hedges took up an active life in politics and public affairs, serving in such posts as territorial superintendent of schools, probate judge, and supreme court reporter.

N. P. Langford credited Hedges with the idea of setting aside the Yellowstone region as a national park. The idea, Langford said, arose as members of the Washburn Expedition sat around a campfire September 19, 1870, after they left the geyser basins. Yellowstone Historian Aubrey L. Haines says Hedges didn't invent the idea, but credits him with supporting it through a series of articles he wrote for the Helena Herald. *Here's Hedges's description of cooking fish on the hook.*

My individual taste led me to fishing, and I venture that none of the party dared to complain they did not have all the fine trout that their several appetites and capacities could provide storage for. Indeed, I felt in gratitude bound to hear testimony that for fine fish, and solid, satisfying fun, there is no body of water under the sun more attractive to the ambitious fisherman than Yellowstone Lake.

While upon the subject of fishing, allow me to relate one or two instances of personal experience. One day, after the loss of one of our comrades, when rations were getting short, I was deputed to lay in a stock of fish to eke our scanty larder on our homeward journey.

Proud of this tribute to my piscatory skill, I endeavored under some difficulties, to justify the expectations of my companions, and in about two hours, while the waves were comparatively quiet, I strewed the beach with about 50 beauties, not one of which would weigh less than two pounds, while the average weight was about three pounds.

Another incident, illustrative of the proximity of hot springs rather than of trouting: Near the southwest corner of the lake is a large basin of exceedingly hot springs. Some are in the very margin of the lake, while others rise under the lake and indicate their locations by steam and ebullition upon the lake's surface when the waves are not too uneasy. One spring of large size, unfathomable depth, sending out a continuous stream of at least 50 inches of scalding water, is still separated from the cool water of the lake by a rocky partition not more than a foot thick in places.

I returned to the narrow rim of this partition and catching sight of some expectant trout lying in easy reach, I solicited their attention to a transfixed grasshopper, and meeting an early and energetic response, I attempted to land my prize beyond the spring, but unfortunately for the fish, he escaped the hook to plunge into this boiling spring.

As soon as possible, I relieved the agonized creature by throwing him out with my pole, and although his contortions were not fully ended, his skin came off and he had all the appearance of being boiled through. The incident, though excusable as an incident, was too shocking to repeat.

— From Cornelius Hedges, "Yellowstone Lake," *Helena Daily Herald* (November 9, 1870).

Describing the Grand Geysers

(1870)—Henry Washburn

"Our usually staid and sober companions threw up their hats and shouted with ecstasy at the sight."

Henry Dana Washburn was the most prominent member of the expedition that bears his name, so it's no surprise that he was elected to lead it. Washburn had a distinguished career as a US Army officer in the Civil War. After the war, he served two terms in the US Congress representing Indiana, but he declined to seek a third term because of failing health. Hoping that life in the West would restore his vigor, Washburn sought and received appointment as surveyor general of Montana in 1869.

Washburn was an able leader who maintained order among the fractious members in the expedition, but the rigors of the trip were hard on his fragile health. He caught a cold when the expedition was delayed south of Yellowstone Lake. He died a few months later, but not before he wrote a series of articles about the trip for the Helena Herald. *Here General Washburn describes the geysers of the Upper Geyser Basin and gives them the names they're known by today.*

Leaving the lake, we moved nearly west, over several high ranges, and camped in the snow amid the mountains. Next day, about noon we struck the Firehole River and camped in Burnt Hole Valley. This is the most remarkable valley we found. Hot springs are almost innumerable. Geysers were spouting in such size and number as to startle all, and are beyond description. Enormous columns of hot water and steam were thrown into the air with a velocity and noise truly amazing. We classified and named some of them according to size:

No. 1. The Giant, 7 by 10 feet, throwing a solid column of water from 80 to 120 feet high.

No. 2. The Giantess, 20 by 30, throwing a solid column and jets from 150 to 200 feet high.

No. 3. Old Faithful, 7 by 8, irregular in shape, a solid column each hour, 75 feet high.

No. 4. Bee Hive, 24 by 15 inches, stream measured 219 feet.

No. 5. Fan Tail, irregular shape, throwing a double stream 60 feet high.

No. 6 is a beautiful arched spray, called by us the Grotto, with several apertures through which, when quiet, one can easily pass, but when in action each making so many vents for the water and steam.

Upon going into camp we observed a small hot spring that had apparently built itself up about three feet. The water was warm but resting very quietly, and we camped within 200 yards of it. While we were eating breakfast this spring, without any warning threw, as if it were the nozzle of an enormous steam-engine, a stream of water into the air 210 feet, and continued doing so for some time, thereby enabling us to measure it, and then as suddenly subsided.

Surrounded by these hot springs is a beautiful cold spring of tolerably fair water. Here we found a beautiful spring or well, raised around it was a border of pure white, carved as if by the hand of a master-workman, the water pure. Looking down into it, one can see the sides white and clear as alabaster, and carved in every conceivable, shape, down, down, until the eye tires in penetrating.

Standing and looking down into the steam and vapor of the crater of the Giantess with the sun upon our back, the shadow is surrounded by a beautiful rainbow; and, by getting the proper angle, the rainbow, surrounding only the head, gives that halo so many painters have vainly tried to give in paintings of the Savior.

Standing near the fountain when in motion, and the sun shining, the scene is grandly magnificent; each of the broken atoms of water shining like so many brilliants, while myriads of rainbows are dancing attendance. No wonder, then, that our usually staid and sober companions threw up their hats and shouted with ecstasy at the sight.

We bid farewell to the geysers, little dreaming there were more beyond. Five miles below Burnt Hole we found the "Lake of Fire and Brimstone." In the valley we found a lake measuring 450 yards in diameter, gently overflowing, that had built itself up by a deposit of white sub-strata at least 50 feet above the plain. This body of water was steaming hot.

— From Henry Washburn, "The Yellowstone Expedition," *Helena Daily Herald* (September 27 and 28, 1870).

Treed by a Lion

(1870)—Truman Everts

A man lost in the wilderness spends a terrifying night up a tree when a mountain lion stalks him.

Probably the best-known story of early travel to Yellowstone Park is Truman Everts's account of being lost and alone there for thirty-seven days. In 1864 Abraham Lincoln appointed Everts to be assessor of internal revenue for Montana Territory, but he lost that job in the political machinations of the Grant administration. Everts decided to return to Vermont and joined the Washburn Expedition to have a final adventure in the West.

Everts became separated from his companions in the Washburn Expedition as they made their way through heavy timber east of Yellowstone Lake. Everts was extremely nearsighted, so he got off his horse to look for tracks. While he was scrutinizing a path, the horse ran away, leaving him only the clothing on his back and items in his pockets. A clever and tenacious man, he built a nest between two hot springs to survive a snowstorm, made fire with the lens from an opera glass, and lived mostly on a diet of thistle roots.

He told about his adventures in an article published by Scribner's Monthly *that helped win support for the creation of Yellowstone National Park. Here's one of those adventures.*

I stretched myself under a tree, and fell asleep. How long I slept I know not; but suddenly I was roused by a loud, shrill scream, like that of a human being in distress. There was no mistaking that fearful voice. It was the screech of a mountain lion; so alarmingly near as to cause every nerve to thrill with terror.

The work of the moment was to yell in return—seize with convulsive grasp the limbs of the friendly tree—and swing myself into it. Scrambling hurriedly from limb to limb, I was soon as near the top as safety would permit.

The savage beast was snuffing and growling below—on the very spot I had just abandoned. I answered every growl with a responsive scream. Terrified at the delay and pawing of the beast, I increased my voice to its utmost volume. I then broke branches from the limbs and madly hurled them at the spot from whence the howlings preceded.

I failed to alarm the animal that now began to make the circuit of the tree—as if to select a spot for springing into it. With my strength increased by terror, I shook the slender trunk until every limb rustled. All in vain. The terrible creature pursued his walk around the tree—lashing the ground with his tail, and prolonging his howling almost to a roar.

It was too dark to see, but the movements of the lion kept me apprised of its position. Whenever I heard it on one side of the tree, I speedily changed to the opposite—an exercise that I could only have performed under the impulse of terror. I would alternately sweat and thrill with horror at the thought of being torn to pieces—and devoured by this formidable monster. All my attempts to frighten it seemed unavailing.

Disheartened at its persistency, and expecting at every moment that it would take the deadly leap. I tried to collect my thoughts, and prepare for the fatal encounter. Just at this moment it occurred to me that I would try silence. Clasping the trunk of the tree with both arms, I sat perfectly still.

The lion ranged around, occasionally snuffing and pausing—all the while filling the forest with the echo of his howling. Suddenly it imitated my example and fell silent. This was more terrible than the clatter and crash of his movements through the brushwood. Now I did not know from what direction to expect this attack. Moments passed with me like hours. After a lapse of time, which I cannot estimate, the beast gave a spring into the thicket and ran screaming into the forest. My deliverance was effected.

Had strength permitted, I should have retained my perch till daylight. But with the consciousness of escape from the jaws of the ferocious brute came a sense of overpowering weakness. That made my descent from the tree both difficult and dangerous. Incredible as it may seem, I lay down in my old bed, and was soon lost in a slumber so profound that I did not awake until after daylight.

— Excerpt from Truman Everts, "Thirty-Seven Days of Peril," *Scribner's Monthly* 3, no. 1 (November 1871): 1–17.

Part 4:
First Tourists

INTRODUCTION

Montana pioneers brave the wilderness to see deep canyons, glass mountains, petrified forests, and boiling geysers.

When the Washburn Expedition returned to civilization late in the summer of 1870, the news that the rumors of wonders on the upper Yellowstone were true spread like wildfire. It was too late in the season for another expedition to a place that could be snowbound by September, but soon people were making plans to see the place for themselves.

The powerful appeal of a wonderland filled with canyons and waterfalls, glass mountains, and geysers was not lost on entrepreneurs who began planning hotels and stage lines. A coalition of Bozeman and Helena businessmen began building a road to Mammoth Hot Springs through the canyon that soon took its name from toll collector Yankee Jim. A similar group from Virginia City commissioned Gilman Sawtell to extend his road from Henry's Lake to the Lower Geyser Basin. The race for tourist dollars was on.

Men who were drawn to the area by the reward offered for rescuing Truman Everts, the man who was lost from the Washburn Expedition for thirty-seven days, saw an opportunity for a hot springs resort at Mammoth Hot Springs. In 1871 Harry Horr and James McCartney took out a 160-acre homestead near the springs and built the first hotel in the park, a one-story, sod-covered cabin. But this crude hotel did have hot and cold running water. A stream of 150-degree water bubbled by one side of the cabin and another of 40 degrees ran on the other. By the time Ferdinand Hayden arrived there with his expedition, he was surprised to find a tourist village at Mammoth Hot Springs.

The easiest access routes to Yellowstone wonders were up the Yellowstone River to Mammoth Hot Springs or up the Madison River to the grand geysers, so most of the early visitors came from Montana. The first tourists were groups of men who traveled light and planned to live off the land, but women were not to be left behind.

In 1872 Hiram and Emma Stone and their two sons were visiting Mammoth Hot Springs, where they hired two men to guide them across the park to the geyser basins on the Firehole. Mrs. Stone rode horseback across the roadless wilderness to become the first woman to make a complete tour of the park.

Yellowstone's First Tourists Seek "First Blood"

(1871)—Calvin C. Clawson

Early tourists encounter bears and shoot bald eagles for fun.

In 1871—a year before the national park was created—a small group of men set off from Virginia City, Montana, "to see Wonderland." The group, considered by many to be Yellowstone's first tourists, was led by US Commissioner of Mines Rossiter Raymond. Their principal chronicler was Calvin C. Clawson, who wrote about the trip in a series of seventeen articles for the New Northwest, *a Deer Lodge, Montana, newspaper.*

Clawson not only described the sights the party encountered, he speculated on such things as using the finely ground minerals found in the geyser basins for lady's cosmetics and embalming bodies in the calcium-laden waters. Clawson also described the antics of men out for an enjoyable adventure. Like groups everywhere, they sometimes entertained themselves with strange contests—like seeing who could get "first blood."

The morning of the eleventh was very pleasant, and a calm air was highly appreciated after a boisterous night. While we made preparations to start, a large eagle sailed over and alighted in a tree half a mile down the creek. Prof. Raymond and Eiler immediately mounted their horses and gave chase.

As yet we had taken no game—not even a chicken killed or a fish caught—and there was a strife among us to see who would get the first blood.

I knew that when we got to Bear Creek, among the berries, with my dog Nig's assistance, I could get a bear—for he was celebrated for hunting that kind of game.

Bear Creek is well named. Its underbrush furnishes bears with ample and secure hiding places. Here berries grow in abundance, and the industrious ant rears her ingenious palace. Bruin is fond of both.

After the horses were unsaddled and secured, in company with the dog and my gun, I took a stroll up the creek to see if we couldn't bag a bruin before the eagle hunters came up. As we advanced, the "signs" became more and more numerous—until I was satisfied we would soon be rewarded with a bear fight.

All of a sudden, I was brought to my senses by a terrible noise in the bushes ahead of me, as of the rushing and snorting of wild animals. Of course, it was a bear out berrying, and he was coming directly towards me. Nearer and nearer he came. I could see the tops of the high berry bushes bending before him.

Now it occurred to me there might be two—two bears are a good many. I would have whistled for Nig, but to attract attention would prove ruinous, for the bear was coming plenty fast already. If the gun should fail, there would be no alternative but to trust to my knife, and that would bring me face to face with the enemy.

Old hunters say a bear can be successfully handled (in an emergency) by waiting till he rises on his hind feet, and then smiting him under the fifth rib till he dies. They never tell how the bear amuses himself in the meantime— whether he "throws up his hand" or goes for his foe "tooth and toe nail."

These things have to be considered—and I considered them. I recollected that I had never seen but one man who stabbed a bear. We had to take two horses to get him (not the bear) to camp—he was too much scattered to carry on one. The best surgical assistance never could make anything else out of him but a torn up man—although he lived.

Closer and closer come the bears—I thought I got a glimpse of them through the bushes. There was a drove of them—two abreast, rushing on me—another minute and the fight would begin. There was no tree in reach. I held a council of war—a change of base was considered in order. I immediately stepped behind a point of rocks half a mile down the creek. After waiting a reasonable time for the enemy to appear, I walked into camp— demoralized, but not damaged. The dog soon followed, panting as though he too had a race for life.

In a short time the eagle hunters made their appearance—with their hats bedecked with trophies in the shape of eagle feathers, and an eagle hanging to the horn of each saddle—while the wings dragged the ground.

The old one had showed fight when she saw the hunters approaching, and settled down by the nest to protect her young. After several shots from a rifle, she was disabled—and Mr. Raymond climbed the tree as far as possible, threw a rope over the limb, and shook the two young out—then brought them to camp. They were monsters for their age, and after admiring them a while, we turned them loose to shift for themselves.

The first blood was unanimously accorded to the professor by the balance of the party, but if the other parent bird had been at home, they might have "got away" with the invaders.

— Clawson's complete account of the 1871 trip to the upper Yellowstone is in Eugene Lee Silliman, ed., *A Ride to the Infernal Regions* (Helena, Montana: Riverbend Publishing, 2003), 42-46.

Saving a Scalded Man

(c. 1872)—Henry "Bird" Calfee

A pioneer photographer saves the life of a friend who has fallen into a geyser.

In his reminiscence about his trip to Yellowstone Park, Henry "Bird" Calfee said, "fabulous report in from the upper Yellowstone region of the existence of astounding wonders" compelled him and his friend, Macon Josey, to visit the area. Calfee's account of their trip was found at the Pioneer Museum of Bozeman in a clipping from an unidentified newspaper, which apparently was published about twenty years after the trip.

Calfee said the trip took place in 1871, but that must be in error, because he recounts things that didn't occur until 1872—like an encounter with the notorious Harlow gang of horse thieves. Calfee was so impressed with the park that he returned often. He became one of Yellowstone's first photographers and eventually started a business selling photographs there. Here's an excerpt from his reminiscence that tells about Josey's fall into a geyser.

While out exploring and gathering specimens on a tributary of the Firehole River we scared a deer out of a small bunch of timber. In its frightened condition, it attempted to bound over a large open geyser that was in its line of retreat. Failing to land with its hind feet on the farther edge of the formation, it fell backwards into the boiling caldron. We hastened to its rescue and attempted to raise it out by thrusting a long pole under its belly. The formation gave way with us, my companion going down with it into the horrible seething pool. I narrowly escaped by falling backward into the solid formation.

I assisted my companion as quickly as possible, but in one-half minute he was scalded from his waist down. He was so a badly scalded that when I pulled his boots and socks off the flesh rolled off with them. I managed to get him back to camp and put what little remaining flour we had on his raw and bleeding burns.

I began immediately making preparations for an early start the next morning for the settlement on the Madison River below. I expected to reach it in two days, but so slow was our progress that we were scarcely out of sight of the Lower Geyser Basin at the end of that time. I hastily constructed a travois after the Indian style, in which Josey could ride.

I then went up to the Old Faithful geyser to whom we had delivered our washing the morning before. I found it all nicely washed and lying on his pearly pavement ready for delivery. Our linen and cotton garments, which had been stiff and black with dirt, lay there as white as the driven snow, and our woolen clothes were as clean as could be. But oh my, imagine them in that mammoth unpatented washing machine boiling for one solid hour and then imagine my 165-pound carcass inside of a suit of underwear scarcely large enough for a ten-year-old boy. I said to Old Faithful, you are a mighty good laundryman but you will not do up my flannels any more. I went back to camp regretting that we couldn't stay in this vicinity long enough to patronize him again.

Early next morning I got up and got breakfast, which was not a very laborious job as it consisted of elk, straight. I saddled and packed up, got Josey into his travois and started down the river reluctantly leaving behind us the world's most marvelous wonders, many of which were yet to be won by human eye. I here resolved to return as soon as circumstances would permit.

We were all day getting into the Lower Geyser Basin, all of ten miles. We camped near the Fountain geyser and as we were leaving next morning, it began spouting. Josey asked me to lead his horse around where he could have a good view of the eruption that continued at least a half hour. Josey declared he could have lain there all day, suffering as he was, and watch such displays of natural magnificence and grandeur. I doubt whether distress and pain could relieve him of all desire for such displays of natural beauty. We bade goodbye to the Fountain and started on our journey.

The next day we traveled along at a better speed. That afternoon we passed through the portals of that picturesque valley of the Madison and shook hands with a hardy pioneer, George Lyon, whose latch string hung outside of his dirt covered mansion. As we rode up he stood in his yard with his ax in his hand silently gazing, full of wonder and amazement at the appearance of such a strange-looking caravan.

Josey perched on his eminence with his head bundled up for protection from mosquitoes with his legs crossed resembling an Arab more than a geyser crippled shoemaker. And I, with my geyser done up clothes, presented a spectacle, which Lyon had never seen before.

We were welcomed, thrice welcomed, to the hospitalities of our host and we were soon off our horses and at home. About the first thing I did was to introduce Josey to a cake of soap and a trough of water, after which there was little resemblance to the man that started out with me in the spring to explore the wonders of Yellowstone.

Our landlord soon spread out a bountiful supper—the best that a bachelor's culinary affords. After supper, we sat around his open fireplace and narrated for the first time our perilous adventures. He listened attentively to all we said and pronounced us lucky to be alive.

— Abridged from Henry "Bird" Calfee, "Calfee's Adventures," undated newspaper clipping, Pioneer Museum of Bozeman.

A Million Billion Barrels of Hot Water

(1872)—Harry J. Norton

A man washing dishes is surprised when a geyser swallows the cutlery.

A group of professionals and businessmen visited the geysers in 1872—long before the era of hot water heaters. The trip was chronicled by Harry Norton, a newspaperman who published the first Yellowstone Park travel guide in Virginia City in 1873. Norton's Wonderland Illustrated; or, Horseback Rides Through the Yellowstone National Park, *described not only the sights, but also his travel companions and their antics. Norton called one of his friends, who owned telegraph lines between Deer Lodge and Bozeman, "Prince Telegraph." Here's Norton's description of the Prince's experiments in geyserland.*

Just for the oddity of the idea, some of the party proposed that we should try a cup of geyser tea. Happy thought! A million billion barrels of hot water within easy reach, and nothing to do but put the tea a-drawing! Notwithstanding all that has been said by former tourists, the tea was excellent—and produced no disagreeable effects.

We afterwards utilized several of the geysers by boiling meat, dirty clothes, beans, coffee, etc., each experiment being attended with satisfaction. For boiled beans, two quarts of "navies" were put in a flour sack, and with a rope, lowered into the steaming crater. In thirty minutes, they were perfectly soft and palatable. This is not a first-rate method to make allopathic bean soup, but for a homeopathic dose, it can't be beat. In this connection, a little incident:

Prince Telegraph's wardrobe, like our saddle-seat, was constantly getting out of repair—and as he had failed in trying to sew on a patch with a needle-gun, he was obliged to procure assistance. He finally compromised affairs by

Early travelers who visited the Upper Geyser Basin used the abundant hot water to make tea, cook food, and wash clothing. NATIONAL PARK SERVICE

a change of duties: Woodall, an expert, was to sew on the patch while Prince Telegraph washed the dishes—his first attempt probably in a lifetime. Hesitating a moment, a brilliant idea struck him. Fifty or sixty feet distant was a very noisy little geyser. Its aperture was in the center of a noisy shallow, well-rimmed basin of about two and a half by four feet. The water scarcely ever covered the flat bottom at a greater depth than two inches.

Pitching the soiled tinware, knives, forks, towels, etc., into a champagne basket, and with an "Oh, ho! I guess I can't wash dishes!" the Prince approaching his improvised dishpan, unceremoniously dumped them in to soak while he placidly enjoyed his meerschaum. Suddenly, and as if resenting the insult to its dignity, the little spouter spit the basin full to overflowing in a second. Setting the contents in a perfect whirl, and the next instant, drawing in its breath, the geyser commenced sucking everything toward the aperture.

We at the camp heard an agonizing cry for help, and looking out, beheld the Prince—with hat off and eyes peeled—dancing around his dishpan in a frantic attempt to save the last culinary outfit. It was comical in the extreme. There would be a plunge of the hand in the boiling water, a yell of pain, and out would come a spoon—another plunge and yell, and a tin plate—an "Oh! ah! o-o-o, e-e-e" and a fork. As we arrived, the towel and one tin plate were just going out of sight; while the Prince, gazing at his parboiled hands, was profanely discussing the idea of being "sucked in" by a geyser!

— From Harry J. Norton, *Wonderland Illustrated:* or, *Horseback Rides Through the Yellowstone National Park* (Virginia City, Montana: Harry J. Norton, 1873), 24–25.

Doughnuts Fried in Bear Grease

(1873)—Sarah Tracy

Despite an Indian scare, a woman tours Yellowstone and has a boat named for her.

Indians stole a band of horses the night before Sarah Tracy left Bozeman for Yellowstone Park in June 1873. But Mrs. Tracy was used to Indians. When she arrived in Bozeman in 1869 with her new husband, Bozeman pioneer W. H. Tracy, Indians were encamped on the south of town. Such encounters left Mrs. Tracy with little fear of Indians, but the commander at nearby Fort Ellis didn't want to let her party go in the midst of "Indian troubles." After some haggling, he finally agreed to provide an armed escort. Here's Sarah's reminiscence about the trip.

The night before leaving home the Crow Indians made a little stealing escapade in town, coming past the garrisoned fort at Ellis and driving off a band of horses. The alarm was given shortly after midnight and a company of citizens started in pursuit soon to be joined by the soldiers from the fort.

Early in the morning, we started with the four-horse stagecoach. When we got to the fort, the commanding officers would not let us proceed further on account of the Indian scare. But after some talk the driver asked for an escort, which was granted, and we were soon on the way with twelve mounted soldiers. Their guns on the shoulder, their belts filled with cartridges, their knapsacks on their shoulders looked war like.

They accompanied us as far as Ferrell's ranch where we stopped for dinner. Seeing no signs of Indians, they started back to the fort and we went on to Bottler's ranch for the night.

It is seventy-five miles from Bozeman to the Mammoth Springs and it took two days of good driving as the roads were then. As we neared the springs, we climbed a very steep mountain from the summit getting a fine, breathtaking view of the wonderful Mammoth Hot Springs. The descent down the mountains required what was known as rough-locking, fastening the rear wheels with log chains as well as the wagon breaks.

We drove up to the hotel with a grand flourish of the four-horse whip bringing the landlord and the guests to the door to meet us. Twenty dollars a week for room and board and five dollars extra for baths was the price. The menu was hardly as elaborate or as well served as one now gets in the large hotel. But we enjoyed every thing. The baths in the primitive tin bathtubs— nature had coated them over with a beautiful white coating making them to rival the modern porcelain ones. Everything was just as nature made it, unmolested by man. No building but the hotel, store and bathhouses.

We climbed the terraces, explored the natural cave, visited the Devil's Kitchen, walked to the river to fish, enjoyed two baths and three hearty meals each day and were ready the next Monday morning to start our horseback through the park. When the remainder of our company came there were fifteen persons in our outfit, Mrs. Graham and I being the only ladies. I had never ridden on horse back before so no little difficulty was experienced in selecting the little grey pony that carried one safely through the park. We rode sidesaddle and it was quite difficult for an amateur rider to keep seated. We had eight packhorses, a riding pony for each person, a guide with his packhorses, a photographer with two pack mules. When we were starting out on the trail, we made quite an imposing appearance.

Our trail crossed the Gardner River four or five times, a very rapid stream with large boulders at the bottom. I was in great fear in crossing but as there was no alternative, I had to hold on as best I could. At first, I dismounted to walk over the bad places but they were so frequent I concluded to remain in the saddle. Our old mountaineer remarked, wait until the mountains are so steep that you must hold on to the horse's ears going up and the tail going down. Some mountains were so steep the saddle would slip over the back going up and nearly over the head coming down.

We made only one ride each day, as it was so much work to pack the horses. The guide was the cook and his cooking utensils as such were used by the campfire. The baking powder bread was mixed in the mouth of the flower sack then baked in the frying pan before the campfire. As soon as sufficiently hardened it was taken out and put against a piece of wood while the frying pan was used to cook the bacon.

We had a coffee pot, some tin plates, cups, tin spoons, a few knives and forks. In the morning, it was very interesting to watch the men do the packing. None but an experienced mountaineer could pack the horses correctly. A peculiar hitch of the ropes call the "diamond hitch" must be used and it took pilgrims a long time to learn it. The bedding was rolled in canvas, one roll on each side of the packsaddle and must be evenly balanced—then the valises, grips and last of all kitchen utensils. One staid old horse had the honor of carrying these on top of his pack. One morning soon after leaving camp it slipped down under him and he commenced to buck. On he went bucking at every step scattering knives forks and spoons far and wide. When he was stopped, we searched and found our implements in a sad condition, both coffee pots jammed so we could hardly use them and many utensils missing.

The trail we followed went first to the Tower Fall, a beautiful fall in Tower Creek. Our next point of interest was the Grand Canyon and Lower Falls of the Yellowstone. We had no easy grade up the mountains to view the falls but a hard long climb but we felt repaid when we viewed the great falls and wonderful canyon. Our trail led around Mount Washburn, the Sulphur Mountain, the mud geysers, and then to Yellowstone Lake.

At the lake, we found Commodore Topping and his partners. They had completed a good-sized sailboat. The Commodore was waiting for ladies to ride in his boat, the first ones to name it. As both our names were Sarah we readily agreed to christen the boat "The Sarah." We had a fine sail across the lake and our pictures taken on board after the name was painted on the side. They had a nice camp and gave us the privilege of making some doughnuts and frying them in bear grease.

We then followed a blazed trail across the Upper Geyser Basin. This trail was blazed by Professor Hayden and party sent by the government to make surveys of the country. A blazed trail is where a tree is cut on one side every half mile. We had to depend largely on the sun for direction. We climbed the steepest mountains over fallen timber—our horses having to jump across fallen trees. Many times the inexperienced ones would fall off their saddles. That was me and then would all have a good laugh but really I only fell off three or four times the entire trip.

The sun clouded in and it commenced raining. We tried to follow the blazed trail but in the pouring rain that followed we got lost entirely. We came toward night to the foot of a very high mountain and made camp, wet through, tired and hungry. I stood by the campfire to dry my clothes. My dress had a long polonaise of calico and when it got dry, caught fire and the whole back was burned off. We made camp on the wet grounds, slept in our wet bedding, awoke refreshed to climb the mountain, and got a fine view of the Upper Geyser Basin.

Coming in near Old Faithful, we camped a few days to see the grand display, all the natural formations undisturbed by the hand of man. We came down through the Lower Basin and camped for lunch at the Devil's Paint pots as they were then called. We thought them wonderful. Then we passed Hells Half Acre, now called the Excelsior Geyser, and returned to Mammoth Springs Hotel.

We were gone twelve days and all thought that bacon and bear grease doughnuts had certainly agreed with us, and the balmy breezes and the mountain sunshine had done complexions to a turn. While our clothing was a little the worse for wear yet we had seen the Yellowstone National Park in its primitive beauty.

— Sarah Tracy's reminiscence is at the Museum of the Rockies in Bozeman.

Dolly Saved My Life

(1874)—Mabel Cross Osmond

An alert horse saves the life of a six-year-old girl.

Mabel Cross Osmond was just six and a half years old when she first went to Yellowstone Park with her parents in 1874. Mabel's father, Captain Robert Cross, was a Civil War veteran who came to Montana to be the post trader at Crow Agency, which was then located nine miles east of the present Livingston, Montana. Mabel wrote her memoir more that fifty years after her trip, but she still had vivid memories of it. Here's an abridged version.

It was in the summer of 1874 that my father decided on our trip through Yellowstone Park before returning to our home in Des Moines. He had been in the park before while out with a half-breed scout on a government mission to the Bannocks, but how far he had been, I do not know.

Careful preparations were necessary for our undertaking as it was most unusual for a woman to make the trip and never before had a child been there. I was then six and a half years old. My father had a special saddle made for me—as of course, we all rode horseback. The blacksmith, taking a man's saddle, fastened a covered iron rod from the pommel around on the right side to the back. This rod and the seat were well padded with blankets. A covered stirrup, wide enough for my two feet was hung on the left side and across this open side from the pommel to the rod in back was attached a buckled leather strap so that, when mounted, I sat as a child in a high chair.

My dun-colored Indian pony, named "Dolly" was found most trustworthy, saving my life by instantly stopping when, while descending a steep trail my saddle turned, leaving me hanging head downward, helplessly strapped in until the others could reach me. At first my father had a leading rope on her, but after two or three days that was found unnecessary as she followed his horse everywhere, climbing the steepest trails and through the streams, swimming the Yellowstone on our return trip.

On starting one bright morning early in July, we rode in an agency wagon with an armed escort for the first day out. This was found to be a wise precaution, for the following day on this same road between the agency and the ford two men were attacked and killed by the Sioux.

I think our first day's ride took us to the Bottler ranch—anyway it was here that our escort turned back after seeing-us over the most dangerous part of the trip. And here we enjoyed one of "Grandma" Bottler's good dinners. I remember the cute little roast pig with an ear of corn in its mouth, and also being awakened during the night by hearing her shrilly shouting—"Fredereek, Fredereek, the skunk is after the chickuns." Though eighty years old, she kept her "store teeth" put away—"fearing to wear them out"—she told us.

There was at that time no road into the park except from Virginia City and we were entering from the north, so we took to the game and Indian trails. Upon reaching Mammoth Hot Springs, we camped in the wooded glen.

My father fashioned a basket out of some stays from mother's corset and laid it in one of the pools of the terraces, where the waters were constantly running and left it until our return. We found it beautifully encrusted with the mineral deposits. This we took back to Iowa along with an interesting collection of which I still have a few specimens.

We could not travel far each day as my mother was not strong and, unfortunately, had a rough riding horse, not the one selected for her, as it had not come in off the range on the last "roundup." After a day's ride when a camping place had been decided upon, a buffalo robe was quickly unpacked and my father would lift her down onto it. There she would rest while we all got busy. The horses were unsaddled and the pack mules relieved of their burdens so they could all be picketed. The cook having started his camp fire, undid the packs, set up the oven and prepared the bread for baking and then attended to the fish, or game, and the rest of the dinner. Fish were so plentiful that in the small streams the men could straddle from side to side and pick them up in their hands.

In the meantime, the two tents had been set up and robes spread for our beds. My first duty was to pick and feed Dolly handsfull of the long grass growing so abundantly and she always expected this feast. The days were warm and lovely and the nights were cold!—so cold that of mornings the water in the tin wash basin would be frozen from the time one would use it until the next.

One whole day we rode through timber so dense and so tall that we scarcely saw the sky and our horses often had to jump the fallen logs, which nearly covered the ground. The pack mules found it very difficult to get through and one big mule, named Ben, would even get down on his knees to squeeze between the trees.

At the Upper Geyser Basin, we remained several days waiting to see the Giantess in eruption. One night it was surely expected, so a big fire was built of logs. Robes were spread and we watched for several hours. The crater filled and refilled to the brim several times, but it was not until the next afternoon that the eruption commenced. We were in camp some distance away at the edge of the timber. My father, who was off riding, came galloping to camp to tell us. There were no roads, or signs of any kind to give warning, so as he rode across the crusty formation, his horse broke through. He jumped off his horse, fortunately striking firm ground, and jerked his horse after him. When he looked back down the hole, he could see no bottom.

Of course we watched Old Faithful several times and collected some of the small, smooth pebbles which fell with the water into the pools. One time, the wind veering quickly, my mother was slightly burned by the hot water that struck her arm and shoulder.

We went to Yellowstone Lake and camped on the shore with two men who claimed to be government trappers. They had a small sailboat and took us for a ride to a small island where we found delicious ripe red raspberries and gooseberries. Nothing ever tasted better. I recall on returning, the lake was rough and there was considerable "tacking" necessary, and much rocking of the boat so I became quite seasick.

While visiting the falls, we went out onto the ledge overlooking the Lower Fall. After fastening one end of a long rope to a tree and the other end around his waist, my father carried me onto the ledge. I remember my mother remaining farther back with closed eyes.

Crossing Mount Washburn, we saw our only bear, a black one. My father took a shot at it, but it ran into the woods. We also saw way off in a valley, a large herd of buffalo.

At Tower Fall, we climbed down and stood back of that big boulder. It was here that my mother came near a serious accident. She was climbing down ahead of us, [and while] holding to a branch, it gave way and she slid down some distance before a tree fortunately stopped her. We returned to Mammoth Hot Springs and then over the trail northward and across the Yellowstone River to the Crow Agency.

It was on our way out that we encountered our only sight of Indians being near by. I can still feel a thrill as we caught sight of a dog on the crest of a hill ahead of us. A dog in that wilderness meant Indians were near. The men hastily unslung their guns—their braces of pistols and belt of cartridges they always wore—and proceeded cautiously up the trail, but when we reached the top of the hill, the dog was gone. My father never seemed to fear the Indians, but my mother was always deadly afraid of them, even our own friendly Crows.

I remember my father saying we were twenty-four days in the saddle, riding about 550 miles.

— Abridged from a typescript of Mabel Cross Osmond's reminiscence at the Gallatin History Museum.

PART 5:
TOURISTS FROM AFAR

INTRODUCTION

European royalty, army generals, and tourists from "the states" cross the continent to see "Wonderland."

Most early Yellowstone tourists came from the adjacent territories, because getting to the park was too expensive for other people. But a few wealthy adventurers from distant places made the long trip on America's first transcontinental railroad, which the Union Pacific completed in 1869. But the Union Pacific's nearest stop was at Corrine, Utah, which left an arduous 300-mile stagecoach ride to the west entrance of the park. A few took a steamboat up the Missouri to the world's most inland port, Fort Benton, Montana, which also left a 300-mile stagecoach ride.

Despite the hardships, the Yellowstone "Wonderland" came to the attention of European nobility. Lord William Blackmore accompanied the second Hayden Expedition in 1872 and apparently spread the word when he returned to Europe. In 1874 an Irish peer, the Earl of Dunraven, mounted a hunting expedition to the Rocky Mountains and spent several weeks in Yellowstone Park. Dunraven's book, The Great Divide, *circulated widely in the United States and Europe and helped ignite public interest in the new park.*

Beginning with Colonel W. F. Raynold's 1860 account of mountain man Jim Bridger's descriptions of the area that became Yellowstone National Park, a number of official reports began to pile up. Probably these reports stimulated top army officers' interest in the area.

In 1875, US Secretary of War William Belknap organized a Yellowstone expedition that included five army generals. The officers crossed the country in a plush Pullman car smoking cigars, drinking whiskey, and swapping stories. All through the trip the generals were treated like royalty—they were greeted by silver coronet bands and wined and dined, and speeches were made in their honor. A troop of twenty-four enlisted men and four noncommissioned officers attended the generals' every whim while they made their way through the park hunting, fishing, and seeing the sights. In contrast, in 1877 when General William Tecumseh Sherman visited the park, his party was only a dozen men including his son, two colonels, four enlisted men, and four civilians.

While the Northern Pacific inched its way toward Yellowstone Park, the Union Pacific began building a spur northward toward Yellowstone Park. In 1883 the railroads reached Montana and opened the park to ordinary tourists.

A Dark and Stormy Night in Yellowstone Park

(1874)—The Earl of Dunraven

*An Irish nobleman waits by the campfire
while his friends search for a lost man.*

*The Earl of Dunraven was hunting in Yellowstone in 1874. (It was legal then.)
When a storm came up, the earl and his guides, Fred Bottler and Texas Jack Omo-
hundro, decided to return to camp, but their companion, Dr. George Kingsley,
decided to keep hunting a little longer. The storm grew worse as darkness fell. Here's
the earl's story about what happened next.*

When Jack and I got in we found camp in a sorry plight, everything soaked
through—tents, bedding, and all, and our prospects for the night looked anything but cheerful; but by extending the hide of the wapiti stag between four
trees, and hauling it out taut with ropes, we managed to make a tolerable
shelter; and, taking from out of our cache some dry birch bark and splinters
of fat pine, we lit a huge fire, and sat down to make some tea for supper.

About dusk, we heard a shot, and visions of fresh venison steaks floated
before our eyes. About half an hour passed, but no venison and no Kingsley
appeared, and then we heard another shot, and two or three minutes afterwards yet another.

By this time, it was getting quite dark, and we were puzzled to know
what Kingsley could be firing at—unless, indeed, he was treed by a bear. After
a short interval we heard the sound of his rifle again, evidently further off,
and then it suddenly occurred to us that he was lost and making signals. We
fired our rifles, and whooped, and yelled, and shouted, but all to no purpose.
The sound of his rifle became fainter and fainter—he was going in the wrong
direction.

To be left out on such a night might cost a man his life, for it would have been hard for even an old experienced mountain man to have found material dry enough to make a fire; so Jack and Bottler started out into the blackness of the night and the thick fog to look for him, leaving me behind to heap logs on the fire, and occasionally emit a dismal yell to keep them acquainted with the whereabouts of camp.

For some time I could hear the responsive shouts of the searchers, but after awhile they ceased, and nothing broke the horrid silence except the noises of the night and of the storm.

The heavy raindrops pattered incessantly on the elk hide; the water trickled and splashed, and gurgled down the hillside in a thousand muddy rills and miniature cascades. The night was very dark, but not so black but that I could dimly see white ghost-like shreds of vapor and great indistinct rolling masses of fog driving up the valley in the gale. The wind rumbled in the caverns of the cliffs, shrieked and whistled shrilly among the dead pine trees, and fiercely shook the frail shelter overhead, dashing the raindrops in my face.

Every now and then the fire would burn up bright, casting a fitful gleam out into the damp darkness, and lighting up the bare jaws and white skulls of the two elk-heads, which seemed to grin derisively at me out of the gloom; and then, quenched by the hissing rain, it would sink down into a dull red glow.

My dog moved uneasily about, now pressing close up against me, shivering with cold and fear, nestling up to me for protection, and looking into my face for that comfort, which I had not in me to give him—now starting to his feet, whimpering, and scared when some great gust smote the pine tree overhead, angrily seized and rattled the elk-hide, scooping up firebrands and tossing them in the air.

The tall firs bowed like bulrushes before the storm, swaying to and fro, bending their lofty heads like bows and flinging them up again erect, smiting their great boughs together in agony, groaning and complaining, yet fiercely fighting with the tempest.

At intervals, when the gale paused for a moment as it were to gather strength, its shrill shrieking subdued to a dismal groan, there was occasionally heard with startling distinctness, through the continuous distant din and clamor of the night, a long, painfully-rending cr-r-r-rash, followed by a dull heavy thud, notifying the fall of some monarch of the woods, and making my heart quake within me as I uneasily glanced at the two tall hemlocks overhead that wrathfully ground their trunks together, and whose creaking limbs were wrestling manfully with the storm.

Strange and indistinct noises would come up from the vale: rocks became detached, and thundered down the far-off crags. A sudden burst of wind would bear upon me the roar of the torrent below with such clearness that it sounded as though it were close at hand. It was an awful night, in the strictest sense of the word. The Demon of the Tempest was abroad in his anger, yelling down the valley, dashing out the water-floods with his hands, laying waste the forest, and filling with dread the hearts of man and beast and every living thing.

There was not a star or a gleam of moonlight. It was very gruesome sitting there all alone, and I began to feel, like David, "horribly afraid." I do not know how long I was alone; probably it was only for a short time—a couple of hours or so, at most—but the minutes were as hours to me.

Most dismal was my condition; and I could not even resort to the Dutch expedient for importing courage, to supply my natural allowance of that quality which had quickly oozed out of my cold fingertips. I had poured into a tin pannikin the last drain of whiskey from the keg, and had placed it carefully to settle.

I knew that Kingsley would really want it, so I could not seek consolation in that way. I could not find even a piece of dry tobacco wherewith to comfort myself; I began to feel very wretched indeed; and it was truly a great relief when I heard the shouts of the returning party.

They brought in the lost man pretty well exhausted, for he had been out a long time exposed to the weather, had walked a great distance, and had fallen about terribly in the darkness. He had tried in vain to make a fire, and was wandering about without an idea of the direction in which camp lay.

He was indeed in real need of a stimulant, and when, in answer to his inquiring glance at the keg, I said that there was half a pannikin full, his face beamed with a cheerful smile. But alas! A catastrophe had occurred. A gust of wind or a falling branch had over-thrown all my arrangements, and when I arose to give him the pannikin, behold, it was bottom upwards and dry!

— Excerpt from the Earl of Dunraven, *The Great Divide: Travels in the Upper Yellowstone in the Summer of 1874* (London: Chatto and Windus, Piccadilly, 1876), 174–177.

In a Country Swarming with Grizzlies

(1874)—George Henry Kingsley

An English physician carrying only a small rifle encounters a grizzly.

George Henry Kingsley, an English physician and adventurer, accompanied the Earl of Dunraven on his 1874 tour of Yellowstone National Park. After Dr. Kingsley's death, his daughter, Mary Henrietta Kingsley, compiled his papers into a book entitled Notes on Sport and Travel. *Here's Dr. Kingley's account of hunting grizzlies in Yellowstone Park in 1874, from that book.*

We have had very poor sport, for though we have been in a country swarming with grizzly bears we have only killed one. I was mousing around by myself the other day with the little Ballard (a little, single-barreled rifle) and hearing something smashing about in the willow beds, and thinking that it might be a deer, I proceeded quietly to investigate, when out there lounged the great-grandfather of all the grizzlies.

He looked at me for a moment, and then turned and trotted off, and I trotted after him, when he, being suddenly struck with the idea that valor was the better part of discretion, faced round and walked straight at me, stopping about thirty yards off.

As I only had the Ballard, and was quite out in the open, away from any decently sized trees, I hardly knew what to do. We stood facing each other thus for a few moments, and I could plainly see his pink tongue licking his lips, and his bright little eyes twinkling with rage.

I put up the rifle, but could not cover any part of him where a ball would have been mortal, and if I had only wounded him, he would have been at me in a brace of shakes. After interviewing one another thus, he said "hough" and decided to advance, and I decided to retreat, which I did with considerable decision up the thickest sapling in the neighborhood, hoping, however, that he would follow me at least to the foot of it.

I was in no small state of exultation at the prospect of killing my bear single-handed, but before I was settled, he swerved and went crashing away through the willows, and I saw him no more. He looked as big as an ox.

Texas Jack quizzed me tremendously about this on my return, but the very next day he came back to camp with a far-away look in his eye and requested whiskey. He too had come across a grizzly. He found him in a patch of trees, covering up the carcass of an elk. (They are wonderfully cunning, these bears, and will plaster mud and moss over carcasses they don't want at once, will even plaster over their wounds when they have been shot.)

Jack fired. Hit him. The bear gave one tremendous yell—looked round a moment—then tore up the ground like mad and flew at the trees, sending the bark flying in all directions. Jack lay as flat as a flounder behind a tree, and when, at length, the bear made off, came home a wiser man.

After hearing his account I was rather glad, on the whole, that my friend had not followed to the foot of my sapling, for had I not killed him first shot, he would certainly have made it a very shaky perch to reload on.

— Excerpt from George Henry Kingsley, *Notes on Sport and Travel* (New York: MacMillan, 1900), 161–163.

Stagecoach Driver Bargains for "One Good Square Drink"

(1875)—General W. E. Strong

A drunken stagecoach driver takes his passengers on a wild ride.

Before the Northern Pacific completed its transcontinental link in 1883, the best way from the East Coast to Yellowstone Park was to take the Union Pacific to Corinne, Utah, and then travel north 300 miles by stagecoach. The stagecoach ride itself could be a great adventure. Here's General W. E. Strong's description of his ride in 1875.

At 6 o'clock we were ready to start. The coach had pulled up at the village of Franklin, near Corinne, Utah, and stopped near a whiskey shop for the regular driver to take the reins. This dignitary, who soon appeared, was a slim-built man of five-and-thirty—and so very drunk that I could hardly believe we were to be conducted over our first run by a person in his condition. He had most remarkable control over his legs and hands, however, he managed to reach the coach and climb to his seat without aid from anyone.

"Are you ready," says the driver. "All ready" was the response. Then gathering the reins carefully in his left hand and swinging his whip with the right, the lash cutting sharply across the flanks of the leaders, Lee Goddard, (that was his name) exclaimed, "Git out of here, you pirates." The next instant we were off, lead, swing, and wheel horses on the keen jump. Again and again the whip was applied and thus we departed from Franklin at the rate of sixteen miles an hour.

The intense pleasure to me of this first morning's ride in the great, swaying Concord wagon is indescribable. We were fairly afloat on the great plains of Idaho.

At Bear River we jumped out and stretched our legs while a fresh relay of six handsome bays were hitched to the coach, and in five minutes were bowling along again, at a killing pace. Goddard's run is to Port Neuf Canyon, sixty miles, and he changes five times—an average of 12 miles for each relay.

From Bear River to Port Neuf Canyon the road was fearfully dusty, so we were enveloped in great clouds hour after hour, and it seemed sometimes as though we would surely suffocate. For miles and miles the lead horses were entirely hidden and very frequently all of the horses were lost of view.

The stage driver looked longingly at the demijohn of whiskey—about a gallon—that was under our feet, and finally mustered the courage to say that if he had one good, square drink he was sure he could get through to Port Neuf in time; but as the small flask we carried—strictly for medical purposes—would not probably have come up to his estimate of a good, square drink, I declined the proposition.

Later, and while we were making some sharp curves, where the narrow road was cut out from the mountain's side, with frightful precipices below us, I turned, and, to my astonishment, saw the driver nodding, with the reins hanging loosely in his hands. The situation was by no means pleasant. The horses were going rapidly, with a drunken driver fast asleep, and only a foot between the outer wheels and the brink of the precipice 200 feet high— where, if a horse slipped and went down, or a wheel came off, there was no hope for us.

In view of this, I grasped the reins, and at the same time shook the fellow gently until he awoke, when he very coolly asked, "Wha-ze matter?" and I told him he was sleeping, he laughed saying, "Don't be skeert, ole fellar; them hosses, they knows the road, sure's yer borned. Never upset a stage in my life." At the same time he applied the whip to the swing horses sending us along faster than ever.

— Excerpt from General W. E. Strong, *A Trip to the Yellowstone National Park in July, August, and September* (Washington DC: Government Printing Office, 1876), 15–18.

After railroads arrived at the edges of Yellowstone Park in the 1880s, four-horse coaches shuttled tourists quickly between sights. NATIONAL PARK SERVICE

A General Visits despite
Indian Trouble

(1877)—William Tecumseh Sherman

*A famous Civil War general barely misses
the hostile Indians in Yellowstone Park.*

During the summer of 1877, William Tecumseh Sherman, who was then commanding general of the US Army, decided to tour the forts along the proposed route of the Northern Pacific Railroad. That was just one year after a coalition of Sioux and Cheyenne decimated the Seventh Cavalry under George Armstrong Custer at the Battle of the Little Big Horn. In fact the army was still patrolling the northern plains after the Sioux Chief Sitting Bull fled to Canada. In addition, several bands of Nez Perce refused to move to a reservation in Washington.

Like many military officers, Sherman was fascinated with Yellowstone Park and had read several army and civilian reports about it. He knew about the Nez Perce troubles, but he still decided to take a side trip to see the wonders of Yellowstone Park anyway. He was convinced that the Indians would not enter the park because they feared the geothermal features, so he felt comfortable traveling with a small party of a dozen men. After a fifteen-day tour, Sherman and his companions returned to Fort Ellis, near Bozeman, Montana, just a few days before the Nez Perce entered the park. Had the Indians captured him, it would have changed history.

Here's an abridged version of Sherman's report of his trip to Yellowstone Park.

I suppose you want to hear something of the National Park, or "Wonderland," as it is called here. As you know, I came from the Big Horn here with two light spring-wagons and one light wagon, with six saddle horses. Here we organized the party: Colonels Poe, Bacon, my son and self, three drivers, one packer, four soldiers, and five pack mules; making four officers, four soldiers, one citizen, and twenty-three animals. The packer was also guide.

Our rate of travel was about 20 miles a day or less. Our first day's travel took us southeast over the mountain range to the valley of the Yellowstone; the next two days up the valley of the Yellowstone to the mouth of Gardner's River. Thus far we took our carriages, and along the valley found scattered ranchos, at a few of which were fields of potatoes, wheat, and oats, with cattle and horses.

At the mouth of Gardner's River begins the park, and up to that point the road is comparatively easy and good, but here begins the real labor; nothing but a narrow trail, with mountains and ravines so sharp and steep that every prudent horseman will lead instead of ride his horse, and the actual labor is hard.

The next day is consumed in slowly toiling up Mount Washburn, the last thousand feet of ascent on foot. This is the summit so graphically described by Lord Dunraven in his most excellent book recently published under the title of *The Great Divide*. The view is simply sublime, worth the labor of reaching it once, but not twice. I do not propose to try it again.

Descending Mount Washburn, by a trail through woods, one emerges into the meadows or springs out of which Cascade Creek takes its water; and following it to near its mouth you camp, and walk to the great falls and the head of the Yellowstone Canyon. In grandeur, majesty, coloring, etc., these probably equal any on earth. The painting by Moran in the Capitol is good, but painting and words are unequal to the subject. They must be seen to be appreciated and felt.

The next day, eight miles up from the falls, we came to Sulphur Mountain, a bare, naked, repulsive hill, but of large extent, at the base of which were hot bubbling springs, with all the ground crisp with sulphur; and six miles farther up, or south, close to the Yellowstone, we reached and camped at Mud Springs.

From the Mud Springs the trail leads due west, crosses the mountain range to the Lower Geyser Basin. It would require a volume to describe these geysers in detail. It must suffice now for me to say that the Lower Geyser Basin presents a series of hot springs or basins of water coming up from below, hot enough to scald your hand, boil a ham, egg, or anything else; clear as crystal, with basins of every conceivable shape, from the size of a quill to actual lakes a hundred yards across. In walking among and around them, one feels that in a moment he may break through and be lost in a species of hell.

Six miles higher up the Firehole River is the Upper Geyser Basin—the "spouting geysers," the real object and aim of our visit. To describe these in detail would surpass my ability, or the compass of a letter. They have been described by Lieutenant Doane, Hayden, Strong, Lord Dunraven, and many others. The map by Major Ludlow, of the Engineers, locates the several geysers accurately. We reached the Upper Geyser Basin at twelve noon, one day, and remained there till 4 p.m. of the next. During that time we saw Old Faithful perform at intervals varying from 62 minutes to 80 minutes.

Each eruption was similar, preceeded by about five minutes of sputtering, and then would arise a column of hot water, steaming and smoking, to the height of 125 or 130 feet, the steam going a hundred or more feet higher, according to the state of the wind. It was difficult to say where the water ended and steam began; and this must be the reason why different observers have reported different results. The whole performance lasts about five minutes, when the column of water gradually sinks, and the spring resumes its normal state of rest.

This is but one of some twenty of the active geysers of this basin. For the time we remained we were lucky, for we saw the Beehive twice in eruption, the Riverside and Fan each once. The Castle and Grotto were repeatedly in agitation, though their jets did not rise more than 20 feet. We did not see the Giant or the Grand in eruption, but they seemed busy enough in bubbling and boiling.

In our return trip we again visited points of most interest and some new ones. The trip is a hard one and cannot be softened. The United States has reserved this park, but has spent not a dollar in its care or development. The paths are mere Indian trails, in some places as bad as bad can be. There is little game in the park now; we saw two bear, two elk, and about a dozen deer and antelope, but killed none. A few sage-chickens and abundance of fish completed all we got to supplement our bacon.

We saw no signs of Indians, and felt at no moment more sense of danger than we do here. Some four or five years ago parties swarmed to the park from curiosity, but now the travel is very slack. Two small parties of citizens were in the park with us, and on our return we met several others going in, but all were small.

— Abridged from *Reports of the Inspection Made in the Summer of 1877 by Generals P. H. Sheridan and W. T. Sherman* (Washington, DC: Government Printing Office, 1878), 34–37.

An October Snowstorm

(1880)—Carrie Adell Strahorn

A woman braves snow and cold to join her husband at the Grand Canyon of the Yellowstone.

Carrie Strahorn was an adventurous woman who insisted on traveling with her husband Robert (she called him "Pard") as he traveled the country searching for destinations for the Union Pacific Railroad. Carrie wrote newspaper columns about her adventures and eventually collected them in a book, Fifteen Thousand Miles by Stage.

Despite warnings about winter storms, the Strahorns decided to visit Yellowstone Park in October 1880. Their guide was George Marshall, who operated a stage line between Virginia City, Montana, and a hotel he built at the Lower Geyser Basin. Also, Park Superintendent Philetus Norris accompanied the Strahorns during part of their trip.

The weather was fine when the Strahorns began, but as they returned to Marshall's hotel after visiting the Mammoth Hot Springs, a snowstorm caught them. Here's Carrie's story about that.

The rain changed to snow, and through the storm we saw the disconsolate face of Mr. Marshall, as he stood near the smoldering campfire muttering to himself as if he had become demented. Upon inquiring the cause of his trouble, he said as soon as he saw the snow he went to look for the horses—and they were gone.

"Gone!" we all exclaimed in unison and despair. The horses were gone and we were at the end of our rations with a big storm upon us. The many warnings not to go into the park so late went buzzing through our minds like bumblebees. The snow was several inches deep and falling faster every minute.

As soon as daylight came the men started in search of the horses. I was left all alone in the camp for several hours waiting with my rifle in hand, until after a hard and hurried chase the horses were overtaken and brought back. We knew that we should hurry home as quickly as possible—but to be within five miles and not to see the falls was asking too much. With the return of the horses we resolved at once to go on.

Superintendent Norris thought it was not best for me to go to the falls. The trip must be a hasty one, and the start home not to be delayed longer than possible for fear of continued storm. The snow ceased falling soon after daylight, but the sun did not appear and there was every indication of more snow. Pard was reluctant to leave me, and knew what disappointment lurked in my detention, but he was overruled. With Mr. Norris he started off leaving me with Mr. Marshall—who was to have everything ready for the return to Lower Geyser Basin on their return.

The more I meditated the more I felt that I could not give up seeing the canyon and falls. To be balked by a paltry five or ten miles was more than I could stand. I called to Mr. Marshall to saddle my horse at once for I was going to the falls.

He laughingly said "all right," but he went right on with his work and made no move toward the horse. I had to repeat the request the third time most emphatically and added that I would start out on foot if he did not get my horse without more delay.

He said I could not follow them for I would not know the way, but I reminded him of the freshly fallen snow, and that I could easily follow the trail. He was vexed with my persistence as I was with his resistance, and he finally not only saddled my horse but his own, and rather sulkily remarked that if the bears carried off the whole outfit I would be to blame. When well on our way I persistently urged him to return to the camp and he finally did turn back, but waited and watched me until I turned out of sight.

Alone in the wild woods full of dangerous animals my blood began to cool, and I wondered what I should do if I met a big grizzly who would not give up the trail. The silence of that great forest was appalling and the newly fallen snow made cushions for the horse's feet as I sped noiselessly on. It was a gruesome hour, and to cheer myself I began to sing, and the echoing voice coming back from the treetops was mighty good company.

The five miles seemed to stretch out interminably. When about a mile from the falls other voices fell on my ear, and I drew rein to locate the sound, then gave a glad bound forward for it was Pard on his way back. Mr. Norris said anyone might think that Pard and I had been separated for a month, so glad were we to see each other.

Pard could not restrain his joy that I had followed, and sending the superintendent on to the camp he at once wheeled about and went with me to the falls and canyon that I came so near missing. Up and down o'er hills and vales we dashed as fast as our horses would carry us until the Upper Fall were reached where we dismounted and went up to the edge of the canyon to get a better view.

These falls are visible from many points along the canyon, and the trail runs close to them and also by the river for several miles, giving the tourist many glimpses of grandeur. Above the Upper Fall the river is a series of sparkling cascades, when suddenly the stream narrows to thirty yards, and the booming cataract rushes over the steep ledge 125 feet and rebounds in fleecy foam of great iridescence.

Midway between the Upper and Lower Fall are the famous crystal cascades of Cascade Creek. The cascade consists of a fall of five feet, followed by one of fifteen into a little grotto between two tall boulders which nearly form an arch at the top. A deep pool is formed at the base where the waters rest for an instant and are then forced to roll from the grotto over a slanting slab of 125 feet to the Yellowstone below.

The river widens to a hundred yards between the falls and flows with a gentle current. The bluffs converge again near the lower falls, the one on the west side bulging out as if to intercept the stream, but the waters held an opening a hundred feet wide, and with a wild roar they dashed over the verge 308 feet. The awful grandeur of the scene, the opening of the grandest canyon in the world at our feet, the raging storm and gathering snow, afforded a picture worth a world of trouble to obtain. The foaming, frothing spray lifted high above the verge of the cataract and rose in a column of fleecy purity. It was grand, indeed. We lay flat upon the ground and peered down, down, down into the deep canyon, and in spite of the snow we could catch glimpses of the fine coloring that decked the mountainsides.

The storm increased and the heavens grew darker every hour, but we pushed on. Moran has been chided for his high coloring of this canyon, but one glimpse of its rare, rich hues would convince the most skeptical that exaggeration is impossible. We longed to stay for days and weeks and hear this great anthem of nature and study its classical and noble accompaniment, but there was a stern decree that we must return, and that without delay.

There was no hope for sightseeing as we kept on our way back to the Lower Geyser Basin. Without giving our horses or ourselves over half an hour to rest at noon, we rode on and on, up hill and down, through woods and plains, fording the Firehole River again and again, until at last the lights of Marshall camp were in sight. The storm had continued all day, turning again from snow to rain in the valley. How tired I was when we rode up to the door. Our forty-mile ride was ended at seven o'clock, but it took three men to get me off my horse.

— Adapted from Carrie Adell Strahorn, "Early Days in Yellowstone," *Fifteen Thousand Miles by Stage* (New York: G. P. Putnam's Sons, 1911), 254–286.

PART 6:
NEZ PERCE ENCOUNTERS

Introduction

Angry Indians and Yellowstone tourists tangle in the park.

The Nez Perce generally lived amicably with whites in Idaho and eastern Washington for most of the 1800s. Then in 1860 gold was discovered on Nez Perce land, and white settlers began moving in. In 1877 the government ordered the Indians onto a tiny reservation, but five bands decided to flee and join their old friends, the Crow, in the buffalo country on the Montana plains.

The army sent soldiers to subdue the defiant Nez Perce, but the Indians resisted and defeated them in several battles. In the most dramatic battle, the army attacked a sleeping Nez Perce camp on the banks of the Big Hole River in southwest Montana. The Indians rallied, drove back the attackers, and then retreated, leaving their equipment, teepees, and at least eighty-nine people dead—many of them women and children.

After the bloody Big Hole Battle, the Nez Perce fled through Yellowstone Park, which was an unexpected move, because people thought Indians feared geysers. At the time, several groups of tourists were in the park. The Nez Perce chiefs wanted to avoid whites, but many young men who were enraged by the army's sneak attack at the Big Hole sought revenge. Groups of these braves patrolled far from the chiefs' supervision and bloodshed erupted when the young men encountered tourists.

After passing through the rugged Yellowstone wilderness, the Nez Perce discovered they were not welcome with the Crow, who had accommodated the whites. They headed north in hopes of joining Sitting Bull and his Sioux in Canada.

After the Nez Perce made their way across the Montana plains, the army caught them in October just forty miles from the Canadian border. After a five-day battle in a winter storm, Chief Joseph made his famous "I will fight no more forever" speech and most of the Nez Perce surrendered. A few under Chief White Bird escaped and made their way to Canada.

Guiding the Nez Perce through Yellowstone Park

(1877)—John Shively

Indians force a prospector to guide them through the park.

The first white man the Nez Perce encountered in Yellowstone Park was John Shively, who was traveling alone. Years before, Shively had prospected for gold in the park, so he was familiar with the area. The Indians drafted Shively to guide them ahead of General O. O. Howard's pursuing army.

Shively was camped near the Lower Geyser Basin when the Nez Perce captured him. He had planned to leave the park with a party of tourists from Radersburg, Montana, that he had met earlier that day. The next day, the Nez Perce accosted the Radersburg group, shot two men, and took two women captive. The women were treated well and later released.

Shively traveled with the Nez Perce for thirteen days and then escaped. (The Indians said they let him go when they arrived at an area they knew.)

Several territorial newspapers reported Shively's adventures, and Edwin J. Stanley synthesized them into a single narrative several years later. Here's Stanley's version.

On the evening of the second day, after leaving the Radersburg party, I was camped in the Lower Geyser Basin. I was eating my supper, and, on hearing a slight noise, looked up, and, to my astonishment, four Indians in war-paint were standing within ten feet of me, and twenty or thirty more had surrounded me not more than forty feet off.

I sprang for my gun, but was rudely pushed back. I then asked them what Indians they were, and they answered "Sioux." I said, "No." Then one of them said, "Nez-Perces." They then commenced to gesticulate wildly, and a loud conversation was kept up between them.

I thought the exhibition of a little bravery might help me, so I folded my arms and told them to shoot, that I was not afraid to die. A brother of Looking-Glass then came up, placed his hand on my heart, and held it there a minute or two, and exclaimed, "Hyas, skookum-tum-tum!" meaning "strong heart" in Chinook. He then said in English, "Come with me," walked a few steps, told me to get on a pony that he pointed out, jumped up behind me, and all started for the main camp, a short distance below.

While this was taking place, the other Indians had taken my gun, blankets, horses—in fact, everything I had. Arriving at the main camp, a council of the chiefs was formed, and I was told to take a seat inside the circle.

They asked me who I was, and what I was doing there. I told them. They asked me if I would show them the best trail leading out of the park to Wind River, where they were going. I told them I would, as I knew all about the country. This seemed to be satisfactory, and the council broke up, and the camp moved up a mile or two, where an encampment for the night was formed.

A robe was given me, and an Indian named Joe was detailed to sleep with me. He spoke very good English; said that I must not attempt to escape; that he would be my friend; that they had come that way to get away from Howard; that the trail by that route to Wind River was not known to them, but other Indians had told them about it, and that if I told them the truth they would not harm me.

As I could not help myself, I promised all they asked, and kept my promise. All the time I was with them, I always showed a willingness to get on or off a horse when they told me; and, if an Indian rode behind me on the horse, I offered no objections, and to this fact I am probably indebted for kind treatment.

After breaking camp the next morning, I was ordered to mount. An Indian mounted behind, and I was started ahead with mounted and armed Indians on each side and behind me. While camped the next day, about noon, the Radersburg party were brought into camp.

Shortly afterward, a march was made toward Yellowstone Lake, I still being kept some distance in the advance. After traveling about a mile, I heard seven distinct shots fired, and supposed all the persons had been killed, but that evening Joe told me that only two men had been shot, and the next morning I saw Mrs. Cowan and Miss Carpenter, and was allowed to speak to them, and we traveled near together all that day.

Through this terrible ordeal, the sisters behaved nobly and with the utmost fortitude, although Mrs. Cowan's mental agony at the thought of her husband wounded, and perhaps dead, and being in the hands of savages, was enough to have driven her distracted. With all their savagery and ferocity, let it be said and remembered to the credit of the Nez-Perces, that these ladies were treated with all respect, and protected from all harm, while their prisoners. The next day, Frank Carpenter and his sisters were permitted to go, and the Indians moved to the Yellowstone River.

The first night of our arrival being quite dark, I slipped out of camp and started for the Mammoth Hot Springs, which I reached after traveling two whole nights and one day. Here I found no one, but did find some potatoes already cooked, which greatly revived me after my long fast—having had nothing to eat from the time of leaving the Indian camp.

I then started for Henderson's ranch, which I found destroyed, but plenty of provisions lying around. I got some eggs, and, while cooking them, Mr. J. W. Schuler of Butte City, who was returning from the Clark's Fork mines, rode up. He kindly gave me his horse to ride, he going on foot. That night, early, we reached Dailey's ranch, where we received the kindest treatment, and Mr. Dailey loaned me a horse on which to ride to Bozeman.

I was with the Indians thirteen days, and was treated very well all the time. They traveled very leisurely, not averaging, for the whole time, more than five miles a day. Joe said they were not afraid of Howard. He also said that they did not intend to return to Idaho, as the agent there, John Hall, was a bad man, and would not give them what was due them; that they would remain somewhere in the Big Horn country, and, if the soldiers came, they would join in with the Sioux and Crows and whip them.

— Excerpt from Edwin J. Stanley, *Rambles in Wonderland* (Nashville: Southern Methodist Publishing House, 1885), 175–178.

Captured by Indians

(1877)—Emma Cowan

A young wife watches in terror while Indians shoot her husband in the head.

Emma Cowan visited Yellowstone Park in 1877—the year the US Army pursued the Nez Perce Indians there. Emma was part of the Radersburg party, which included her husband, her sister, her brother, and several friends. They had been seeing the sights for two weeks when they heard about Indian troubles and decided to return home. They built a bonfire and held a sort of minstrel show to celebrate the night before their departure. They didn't realize that the Indians had already entered the park and spotted their fire.

The next morning a group of Indians entered the camp and demanded food. When the tourists packed their wagons and tried to leave, the Indians formed an escort and followed them. Bloodshed began when they encountered another Indian group. Here's Emma's description of watching Indians shoot her husband in the head.

Every Indian carried a splendid gun, with belts full of cartridges. As the morning sunshine glinted on the polished surface of the gun barrels, a regiment of soldiers could have not looked more formidable. The Indians pretended all the while to be our very good friends, saying that if they should let us go, bad Indians, as they termed them, would kill us.

Suddenly, without warning, shots rang out. Two Indians came dashing down the trail in front of us. My husband was getting off his horse. I wondered what the reason. I soon knew, for he fell as soon as he reached the ground—fell heading downhill. Shots followed and Indian yells, and all was confusion. In less time than it takes to tell it, I was off my horse and by my husband's side . . .

I heard my sister's screams and called to her. She came and crouched by me, as I knelt by his side. I saw he was wounded in the leg above the knee, and by the way the blood spurted out I feared an artery had been severed. He asked for water. I dared not leave him to get it.

I think we both glanced up the hill at the same moment, for he said, "Keep quiet. It won't last long." That thought had flashed through my mind also. Every gun in the whole party of Indians was leveled at us three. I shall never forget the picture, which left an impression that years cannot efface. The holes in those gun barrels looked as big as saucers.

I gave it only a glance, for my attention was drawn to something near at hand. A pressure on my shoulder was drawing me away from my husband. Looking back over my shoulder, I saw an Indian with an immense navy pistol trying to get a shot at my husband's head. Wrenching my arm from his grasp, I leaned over my husband, only to be roughly drawn aside. Another Indian stepped up, a pistol shot rang out, my husband's head fell back, and a red stream trickled down his face from beneath his hat. The warm sunshine, the smell of blood, the horror of it all, a faint remembrance of seeing rocks thrown at his head, my sister's screams, a faint sick feeling, and all was blank.

Two days after their capture, the Indians released Emma, her sister Ida, and her brother Frank. They made their way to Mammoth Hot Springs, where they found help. Emma's husband George survived the shooting. He carried the slug that an Army surgeon dug out of his head as a watch fob for the rest of his life.

— Condensed from Emma Cowan, "Reminiscences of Pioneer Life," *Contributions to the Historical Society of Montana, Volume 4* (1903), 168–173.

In 1901 George and Emma Cowan returned to the spot where Indians shot him and left him for dead, and took her captive. GALLATIN HISTORY MUSEUM

A Wounded Man Crawls to Safety

(1877)—George Cowan

After the Nez Perce shoot a tourist and leave him for dead, the man comes to and crawls twelve miles looking for help.

After the Nez Perce shot George Cowan and left him for dead, he regained consciousness to find himself alone in the wilderness. Despite George's grievous wounds, his first thought was for the safety of his wife, who had been taken captive. Here's his tale of crawling a dozen miles to get help.

In about two hours, I began to come back to life, and as I did so my head felt benumbed. The feeling as near as I can express it was a buzzing, dizziness, and the sensation increased as it grew lighter and lighter. I began to feel soon and then my reason came back to me. My head felt very large, seemingly as large as a mountain, and I mechanically raised my hand and began feeling my face and head. I found my face covered with blood and my hair clotted with blood that had cooled there. I then realized the incidents of the day and remembered the shooting.

I could not at first discover where I was wounded, but after getting the blood out of my eyes and pulling my hat off with hair and skin sticking to the clotted blood, I discovered that I was shot in the face and head. Running my hand over my head, I found great gashes in the scalp, and I then thought the ball had passed entirely through my head some way. Feeling my leg, I found it completely benumbed, but there were no bones broken.

I again felt the intolerable pangs of thirst, raised myself on my elbow, and looked about me. I then found that I was some ten or twelve feet from the place of shooting. This, I thought, accounted for the wounds in the back of my head. As far as I could see, the Indians were all gone and I could hear nothing but the moaning of the wind in the trees.

Standing near me was a little pine tree the boughs of which I could just reach, and grasping one, I pulled myself to my feet. My wounds were painful now. As I raised up I saw an Indian close by me sitting on his pony watching me. As I was hobbling away, I glanced backward and saw him on one knee aiming his gun at me. Then followed a twinging sensation in my left side, and the report of the gun and I dropped forward on my face. The ball had struck me on the side above the hip and came out in front of the abdomen.

I thought that this had "fixed me" beyond hope of recovery and I lay perfectly motionless expecting the Indian to finish the job with the hatchet.

I must have lain here fully twenty minutes expecting to die every moment, and during the time, I think my mind must have dwelt on every incident of our trip. I supposed my wife had been killed. I knew the fate she and Ida would be subjected, and my whole nature was aroused as I thought of it.

Directly I heard Indians talking. They were coming up the trail and I could hear them driving numbers of loose horses. They passed within forty feet of me, but I was unnoticed and they were soon out of hearing. I waited for a few moments, then turned over and took a look around me.

I now took another inventory of my wounds, and in trying to rise found that I could not use either of my lower limbs. They were both paralyzed. I then turned up my face and began crawling by pulling myself with my elbows. I thus managed to get into some willows where I found water, which I drank eagerly, and felt greatly refreshed and strengthened. I now began crawling as before, pulling myself on my breast with my elbows. In this way, I crawled to a little stream of warm water, and raised up on my hands and entered the water. I immediately sank to my shoulders in the mud, and the water came up to my chin.

This would not do, so extricating my hands, I again began crawling as before, and found that I could thus cross it. Having crossed it, I entered the willows on the bank, and began crawling down stream and followed it until I struck the Firehole about a half-mile below where I started from. It was now about one or two o'clock in the morning and being completely exhausted I lay down and rested until daybreak.

At dawn, I again started and crawled until noon, when I again stopped to rest. I had been here but a few moments when I again heard Indians approaching, coming down the trail. They passed within ten feet of me and were soon out of hearing.

I lay here for an hour or so and again resumed my wearisome journey. By nightfall, I had made four or five miles, and I kept on during the night, resting at short intervals.

I kept on down the trail, or rather by the side of it, and Indians kept passing by me every little while, driving ponies as they went. I could hear them approaching and then I would lie down and wait till they passed.

I kept this up until Monday morning, having crossed the Firehole Sunday night, and reached the wagons we had abandoned on Friday. I had crawled about nine miles in sixty hours.

As I reached the wagon, I found my faithful dog, Dido, laying beneath it. I called to her, and she came bounding to me, and covered my face and wounds with caresses. The pleasure of the meeting was mutual.

The buggy was laying upon the ground, all of the spokes having been taken from two of the wheels, and I could search it without rising. I found some rags, but I could find nothing to eat.

It occurred to me that I had spilled some coffee when in camp, on Thursday in the Lower Geyser Basin, and calling my dog we started for it, I crawling as before, and the dog walking by my side. The coffee was four miles distant, but I thought not of that. The only idea was to possess the coffee. I was starving.

While crawling along close to the trail, my dog stopped suddenly and began to growl. I grasped her by the neck, and placed my hand over her nose to keep her from making noise. Peering through the brush, I saw two Indians sitting beneath a tree but a few feet from me. I began moving back cautiously and made a circuit around them, keeping the dog close by me. I thus avoided them, and reached the Lower Geyser Basin on Tuesday night.

Here, as I anticipated, I found some coffee, and a few matches. I found about a handful of coffee, and placing it in an empty can that I had found, I pounded it up fine. I then got some water in another empty can that had contained molasses, and building a fire, I soon had some excellent hot coffee that refreshed me greatly. This was my first refreshment that I had taken in five days and nights.

I remained where I was Tuesday night. No one can imagine my thoughts during that time. I supposed that I was the only one of the party left, unless it be my wife, and the speculations upon her fate almost set me mad. It was horrible. All night long I lay there suffering instead of resting, and I hailed with pleasure the break of day.

I made some more coffee, and drank it, which seemed to give me renewed strength, but as my strength returned I felt more keenly the horrors of my position. I thought now I would crawl to where the East Fork empties into the Firehole River, so calling my dog I began my journey.

I found that I was gradually growing weaker, as I could now crawl but a little ways when I would be compelled to stop and rest. At about a mile and a half distant I came to the place of our first night's camp on entering the basin. Here again, I had to cross the river, but as the water was not deep, I made it without mishap. Here I rested for a few moments, before starting for the timber, which was about a fourth of a mile distant. I got there about two o'clock in the afternoon, and laid down under a tree and some brush close to the road. It was an expiring effort, and having accomplished it I gave myself up for dead.

In about two hours, I heard the sound of horses coming, but I was so completely tired out that I did not care whether they were Indians or not. My dog began to growl, but I did not try to stop her. The horses drew nearer, and approached and stopped. The riders had seen me. I looked up and saw that they were white men. They alighted and came to me, and one of them asked: "Who are you?"

I replied that my name was Cowan, and asked them if any news had been received of my wife. They replied that there had not been, and I then cared for nothing further. I turned from them and would have been glad to have died.

One of them kept talking to me, and asking questions that I cared not to answer, while the other built a fire and made some coffee for me. They told me that they were scouts from Howard's command, and that the troops would reach me some time during the next day. They left me some "hard tack" and a blanket, and went on to the scene of the massacre to find the bodies of the party. After they were gone and I had eaten, my desire for life returned, and it seems the spirit of revenge took complete possession of me. I knew that I would live and I took a solemn vow that I would devote the rest of my life to killing Indians, especially Nez Perce.

I laid there until Thursday afternoon, when I heard the sound of approaching cavalry, and shortly afterwards General Howard and some of his officers rode up to me. In a few minutes, I saw Arnold coming. We grasped hands, but neither spoke for some minutes. I could only gasp: "My wife!"

"No news yet, George," he replied.

— Condensed from Frank D. Carpenter, "George F. Cowan's Account," *The Wonders of Geyserland* (Black Earth, Wisconsin: Burnett & Son, 1878), 141–149.

A Battle with Nez Perce

(1877)—Andrew Weikert

Tourists and Indians trade shots in a blazing gun battle.

Andrew Weikert was touring Yellowstone Park with a group of young men from Helena, Montana, when they spotted the fleeing Nez Perce Indians a few miles south of Mammoth Hot Springs. The group beat a hasty retreat to a thick grove of trees and spent the night hiding. The next morning Weikert and a companion named Wilkie decided to leave the others in camp and see if the Nez Perce had moved on. Here's how Weikert described what happened.

We started back for camp, but we ran against an obstacle that made our hair raise and the blood rush to our faces.

We had gotten into the timber not more than a quarter of a mile when we ran onto a lot of the redskins lying in wait for us. They were under the hill, behind a log, so we did not see them until we got within about seventy-five feet.

I was riding ahead when I saw them raise up their heads from behind the log. I told Wilkie there were Indians ahead and wheeled my horse. At the same time I was getting my gun up ready to fire. Looking back I saw half a dozen guns leveled at me so I made myself small as I could, with my gun across my knees.

Bang! bang! bang! then zip! zip! zip! went the balls, but none struck me that time. I was perfectly cool and self-possessed, but will own up that my hair was standing on end when I first saw them. My horse had made a few more jumps, when bang! they went again.

This time they were a little more successful, for they cut a crease in my shoulder blade about four inches long; it did not break a bone, but splintered my shoulder bone a little. And another ball took a piece out of my gunstock. I then began hugging my horse still closer, if such a thing was possible, when they gave us another volley.

By this time, we were out of range, but the balls flew past thick and fast and we could hear them strike the trees. Now for a race!

I supposed that they had their horses close at hand, but they did not mount them just then. Just at this time, my horse tripped his foot and fell and came near turning a somersault. I went sprawling on the ground directly in front of him.

My shoulder was paining considerably, but I did not have long to remain there, for the "reds" were running up again to get another shot at me. I up and let them have one from my repeater. You ought to have seen them dodge. I did this all in a few seconds, and my horse was on his feet again ready to start. I just put my hand on the horn of the saddle, made a bound into it, and was off.

Wilkie had gotten considerably ahead of me by this time, but I soon made up for lost time. We got back on the prairie again on Alum Creek in the valley, then back in the timber again. The Indians did not follow us. We rode as far as we could, then took it afoot, for the under-brush was so thick that we could hardly get our horses through.

After we got into the timber quite a ways, we halted to take breath and to see what damage was done. Wilkie asked me if I was hurt; I told him judging from the hole in my shirt on the right shoulder, and the way the blood was running in my boot, I thought that there must be a scratch at least.

We examined it and bound it up the best we could. Wilkie, being a safe distance from the Indians, did not get hurt. We looked our horses over, and found them all sound, thank fortune. So we mounted and took our direction for camp, rode as lively as we could in hopes that the reds had not been there so we could warn the boys.

— Excerpt abridged from "Journal of Andrew J. Weikert," *Contributions to the Montana Historical Society, Volume 3* (1900), 159–162.

A Narrow Escape from the Nez Perce

(1877)—Ben Stone

*A camp cook climbs a tree to hide when
hostile Indians arrive at Mammoth Hot Springs.*

*Ben Stone was an African American hired to cook for a group of men from Helena
who toured Yellowstone in August 1877, the year the Nez Perce passed through
there. The Helena party fought a couple of gun battles with Nez Perce scouts. Leaving the body of one of their companions behind, several members of the party made
their way to Mammoth Hot Springs, where there was an incipient resort, and
waited for others to arrive. When two young men failed to show up at Mammoth,
two others went to search for them, leaving Stone, a music teacher named Dietrich,
and a wounded man named Stewart to wait for a ride. Here's how Stone described
what happened next.*

No more of our party, having shown up in the three days after arriving at the
Springs, we were alarmed about them, and Andy Weikert concluded to go
and see if he could find anything of them. James McCartney, proprietor of
the Mammoth Hot Springs, kindly volunteered to go with him.

The next day after they left, an ambulance arrived to take Stewart, Dietrich, and myself to Bozeman. The boys with the ambulance begged Dietrich
to go with them, but he said, with tears in his eyes, "My God! What will Mrs.
Roberts say if I go and leave Joe? Through my inducement he came. What
shall I say when I meet his mother, when she asks me where Joe is?"

Dietrich and I concluded to remain until we heard from Weikert and
McCartney. If Joe or any of the rest of the party were brought in, we wished
to be there to care for them, in case they were wounded. One of the party,
with the ambulance (Jake Stoner), remained with us.

Dietrich and Stoner went down to the Gardner's River fishing, not
returning until three in the afternoon, leaving me to keep house alone at the

Springs. After they returned, I cooked dinner and, after eating, Dietrich and I concluded to go up and take a bath. Stoner said he would go along to look at the Springs, and took his gun with him, as he said, "To knock over a grouse, as grub was getting scarce."

After taking our bath and drinking some of the water out of the Hot Springs, we went back to the house.

Dietrich said: "I'll go down and water and stake the mare for the night."

"All right," I answered, "and while you're gone, I'll keep house."

Taking a seat in the doorway, I felt uneasy. On glancing towards the Springs, I saw Jake Stoner running to the house. I smilingly asked him if he had caught any grouse.

He said: "No, but I've caught something else."

I inquired of him what he had caught, when he said that, while up on top of the Springs, he had caught sight of a large party coming this way.

I replied: "You did! That must be white men. How many did you see?"

"I saw two parties, with about ten persons in each nearly forty yards apart, and traveling very slowly."

I said: "They must be white men. Andy and McCartney have found the boys, and are bringing them in. Of course, they are wounded, and have to travel slowly. I'll go in the house, make a fire, and have grub ready for the boys by the time they get here."

"No," said Jake, "don't do that. We had better cache ourselves in the timber until we know whether they are white men or not."

I replied: "That's a good idea—we'll do that."

He then asked for Dietrich, saying, "I'll warn him, so he can take to timber too."

I told him where Dietrich was, and he went down the flat towards him. I started up the gulch to cache myself. After advancing twenty-five or thirty yards, I took to the timber on my right, and went up in it to a point of rocks overlooking the house, and where I could see both trails approaching the house. After waiting there fifteen or twenty minutes, and the parties not coming, I began to think the boys were a long time coming. I looked out, but could not see anything.

I sat down and waited ten minutes—nothing in sight. I exposed myself in trying to find out if the parties were coming. When I got to where I could see, I descried an object in the distance, in what appeared to be a long white blanket. He dodged around out of sight, as if intending to go behind the Springs. Another appeared closer to me, in what also appeared to be a blanket. He dodged around in the same manner as the former one.

Another soon appeared. I had no doubt that he was an Indian, and I said to myself: "Mr. Stone, it's about time you were traveling!" I "lit out" for timber about one hundred yards up the gulch. While I was waiting to see who were coming, the Indians had worked around and got into the gulch I had to go up, and get to the timber. I had to go within five or six yards of them through the brush. Moving as fast and cautiously as I could, I accidentally stepped on a piece of dead brush, which broke with a loud crash. Some of the Indians heard and one made for me. I then moved very fast, for I knew I had to work for my life, if I did not get to timber soon, I was a dead man.

In a few moments, I found that the Indian would cut me off, as from the crash of breaking twigs I knew he was close to me. I thought I was a dead man, sure, and said: "My God! What shall I do!" Just then, I chanced to run under a tree, with low branches. I took hold of the branches and hoisted myself in, without any expectation of saving my life. I had no more than got into the tree, before an Indian on horseback dashed under it, gazing in every direction for me, and seeming surprised at not seeing the object that made the noise.

After going about ten yards, he stopped his horse, raised his gun up on his arm, and listened for an instant. He then went through an opening out of sight.

I now considered myself perfectly safe, but remained in the tree about two hours.

While in the tree I heard several shots at the house, and saw they had made fires there. I supposed they had burned the buildings.

After the Indians left, Stone decided to make for a ranch north of the park. On the way he met a group of soldiers who were pursuing the Indians. Later he learned that the Indians had killed Dietrich, but other members of the party were safe.

— Abridged from "Two Narrow Escapes from the Clutches of the Red Devils in 1877: His Own Story Told by Benjamin Stone," *Avant Courier,* Bozeman, Montana (September 6, 1877).

PART 7:
TRAVELING ON LAND

INTRODUCTION

Improvements in transportation transformed the Yellowstone experience.

The area that is now Yellowstone Park has undergone several transportation revolutions since it was discovered by Euro-Americans early in the nineteenth century. At first visitors had to traverse a roadless wilderness marked only by game trails that often were blocked by dead-fallen trees strewn like spilled Tinker Toys. But today travel is easy.

At first it was hard to get to the park, because there were no roads leading there. As talk of setting the area aside as a national park intensified in the early 1870s, entrepreneurs solved that problem. Businessmen from Bozeman, Montana, built a road from there to Mammoth Hot Springs, while their counterparts in Virginia City extended an existing road from Henry's Lake to the Lower Geyser Basin. In 1880 the park superintendent built the first road across the park between Mammoth and the Lower Geyser Basin.

In 1883, railroads began delivering tourists to the edge of the park. When the US Army took over administration of the park in 1886, they began building roads. The army engineer said park roads should be the best in America and made that so. Soon comfortable carriages pulled by four-horse teams were speeding tourists from site to site on a five-day tour.

In the 1890s the good roads began attracting "wheelmen," as bicyclists called themselves. By the dawn of the twentieth century, motorists were clamoring for admission to the park, but people feared that the noisy contraptions would scare horses and wildlife, so the park superintendent banned them. Although the ban remained in place until 1915, a few cars did get in by accident or contrivance.

How to Pack a Mule

(1874)—The Earl of Dunraven

"You may curse and swear your level best— but it does not do a bit of good."

In 1874 the Earl of Dunraven went on a hunting trip in the Rocky Mountains that included an extensive visit to Yellowstone National Park. The Earl, a titled Irish peer, wrote a book, The Great Divide, *which included 150 pages about his time in the park. The book circulated widely in Europe and the United States and helped bring "Wonderland" to public consciousness. To honor Dunraven's contributions, surveyors named a mountain for him. When the segment of the Grand Loop Road between Mount Washburn and Mount Dunraven was built in 1879, the pass it crossed also was named for him.*

Early tourists like Dunraven had to brave a roadless wilderness to see the sights of the new Yellowstone National Park. That meant supplies had to be carried by pack animals—often cantankerous mules. Dunraven, who was an astute observer and a droll wit, wrote this description of how to pack a mule.

A man stands on each side of the mule to be operated upon; the saddle, a light wooden frame, is placed on his back and securely girthed. A long rope is looped into proper form and arranged on the saddle. The side packs are then lifted into position on each side of the saddle and tightly fastened. The middle bundle is placed between them—a few spare articles are flung on the top—a tent thrown over all—and the load ready to be secured.

The rope is fixed so the fall is one side and the slack is on the other. Each man places one foot against the animal's ribs. Throwing the whole weight of his body into the effort, each man hauls with all his strength upon the line.

At each jerk, the wretched mule expels an agonized grunt—snaps at the men's shoulders—and probably gives them a sharp pinch, which necessitates immediate retaliation.

Pack mules used by early Yellowstone travelers often were cantankerous like this one that was blindfolded for loading. WILLIAM HENRY JACKSON, NATIONAL PARK SERVICE

The men haul a while, squeezing the poor creature's diaphragm most terrible. Smaller and more wasp like grows his waist—at last not another inch of line can be got in, and the rope is made fast.

"Bueno," cries the muleteer, giving the beast a spank on the behind, which starts it off—teetering about on the tips of its toes like a ballet dancer. Having done with one animal, the packers proceed to the next, and so on through the lot.

While you are busy with the others, Numbers One and Two have occupied themselves in tracing mystic circles in and out—among and round and round several short, stumpy, thickly branching firs—and, having diabolical ingenuity they have twisted, tied, and tangled their trail-ropes into inextricable confusion. They are standing there patiently in their knots.

Number Three has been entrusted with the brittle and perishable articles because she is regarded as a steady and reliable animal of a serious turn of mind. She has acquired a stomachache from the unusual constriction of that organ—and is rolling over and over—flourishing all four legs in the air at once.

You may use language strong enough to split a rock—hot enough to fuse a diamond, without effect. You may curse and swear your "level best"—but it does not do a bit of good. Go on they will, till they kick their packs off. And then they must be caught—the scattered articles gathered together—and the whole operation commenced afresh.

— From the Earl of Dunraven, *The Great Divide: Travels in the Upper Yellowstone in the Summer of 1874* (London: Chatto and Windus, Piccadilly, 1876), 139–141.

Stampeded by an Umbrella

(1885)—George W. Wingate

A ranchman wants to impress the ladies, but he discovers that umbrellas and cayuses don't mix.

General George W. Wingate, a wealthy New Yorker, took his wife and seventeen-year-old daughter to Yellowstone Park in 1885. Although there were roads by then, the Wingates decided to travel on horseback, and the women rode sidesaddle. Here's General Wingate's description of an incident that occurred while the ladies were riding through Paradise Valley north of Yellowstone Park.

Hemmed in on every side by high mountains every breath of air was excluded, while the sun beat into it like a furnace; consequently the ride was very hot and tiresome. The heat was so great that the ladies got out their umbrellas from the wagon and raised them, but slowly with great care, for fear of stampeding the ponies who were not familiar with those refinements. The horses, however, were tired and languid from the heat and paid no attention to them so they rode forward in comfort.

As we reached the end of the valley, where the park branch of the Northern Pacific terminates, a dashing young ranchman rode out from behind some buildings. He had a spirited horse and rode well—and he knew it. Ladies were scarce in the valley, and the opportunity to display his horsemanship and personal graces to two at once was not to be thrown away. So he swung his horse around and rode towards us, making his steed curvet and prance, while he swayed to the motion as easily and gracefully as if in an armchair.

While we were admiring him, a sudden gust of wind came whirling out of a canyon. It caught my daughter's umbrella and instantly turned it inside out, with a loud "crack." At the unwonted sight and sound, our horses roused from their lethargy, simultaneously reared, snorted and bolted in different directions, and at their top speed.

The steed of our gallant ranchman was even more frightened that ours. It ran half a mile with him, and as we last saw him he had all he could do to keep it from dashing into a barbed wire fence. The change from his jaunty air to that of anxiety to keep the horse out of the fence was sudden and ludicrous. I fear his pride had a sad fall.

We could do nothing with the horses until May threw away her umbrella, and even then none of our steeds would approach it. As our guide Fisher said, "umbrellas and cayuses don't agree."

— Adapted from George W. Wingate, "My Trip to Yellowstone," *American Agriculturalist*, 45, no. 5 (May 1886): 204–205.

Army Bicyclists
Visit Yellowstone Park

(1896)—Lieutenant James A. Moss

A soldier endorses the bicycle for army maneuvers after a tour of Yellowstone Park.

One of the best-known photographs of Yellowstone Park shows eight uniformed men standing with their bicycles on Minerva Terrace at Mammoth Hot Springs in 1896. They were members of the Twenty-fifth Infantry, US Army Bicycle Corps, a unit of African-American soldiers with white officers.

The unit from Fort Missoula was on maneuvers to test the utility of bicycle soldiers. By the time they reached Mammoth, the soldiers had already set up relays to demonstrate they could move messages quickly and sneaked up on an army camp to show they could spy silently. They had traversed primitive roads, forded streams, climbed fences, and traveled up to ninety miles a day—with each man hauling more than seventy pounds of food and equipment.

Lieutenant James A. Moss, who was in charge, said the maneuvers demonstrated the "practicability of the bicycle for military purposes, even in a mountainous country. The matter was most thoroughly tested under all possible conditions—we made and broke camp in the rain; we traveled through mud, water, sand, dust, over rocks, ruts, etc.; for we crossed and recrossed mountain ranges, and forded streams, carrying our rations, rifles, ammunition, tents, blankets, extra underwear, medicines, tools, repairing material, cooking-utensils and extra bicycle parts." Moss offered the Spalding bicycle company the letter of endorsement below.

In the summer of 1896 an all-Black unit of the U.S. Army went on maneuvers in Yellowstone Park to prove the feasibility of a bicycle corps. They posed at Mammoth Hot Springs for a photo. NATIONAL PARK SERVICE

Fort Missoula, Mont.
Oct. 15, 1896.
Messrs A. G. SPALDING & BROS.

Gentlemen:

In testing the practicability of the bicycle for military purposes in a mountainous country, the Twenty-fifth U.S. Infantry Bicycle Corps, consisting of eight soldiers commanded by myself, has used Spalding Bicycles exclusively. In making our experiments we have ridden about 1,400 miles, the greater part being over some of the worst roads in the United States. On our 800-mile trip to Yellowstone Park, the Main Divide over the Rocky Mountains was crossed twice, the first time over The Summit, near the Mullan Tunnel, and the second time over the old Mullan Stage Line, now little more than a mere trail, and without doubt one of the worst roads in this country.

As it was our object to thoroughly test the matter under all possible conditions we made and broke camp in the rain; we traveled through mud, water, sand, dust, over rocks, ruts, etc.; we crossed and re-crossed mountain ranges and forded streams, carrying our rations, rifles, ammunition, tents, blankets, extra underwear, medicine, tools, repairing material, cooking utensils and extra bicycle parts. The heaviest bicycle, packed, weighed 86 lbs., and the rider 186 lbs.; total. 272 lbs. The lightest bicycle, packed, weighed 67 lbs., and the rider 135 lbs.; total, 202 lbs. The average weight of the bicycles, packed, was 79.7 lbs., the riders, 157.4 lbs.; the bicycles and riders, 237.1 lbs.

The test was of a most severe nature, and it affords me great pleasure to be able to state the bicycles stood the work extraordinarily well, and are without doubt very fine machines.

Very truly yours,
JAMES A. MOSS,
Second Lieutenant Twenty-fifth U.S. Infantry,
Commander Twenty-fifth U.S. Infantry Bicycle Corps.

— "The Spalding Bicycle in the Army" (advertisement), *League of American Wheelmen Bulletin and Good Roads* 25, no. 5 (January 29, 1897): 121.

Bicycling through Yellowstone

(1896)—C. E. Belknap

A "wheelman" jumps into the bushes to avoid colliding with a bear.

The first bicyclists visited the park in 1881. They rode "ordinaries," ungainly contraptions with tiny rear wheels and front wheels up to sixty inches tall. In 1885 "safety bikes" with equal-size front and rear wheels were invented. By the dawn of the twentieth century "wheelmen," as cyclists called themselves, frequented Yellowstone's fine roads. Here's how one of them described his trip.

From Cinnabar, through the park, the government has graded 170 miles of road and is adding more each year. The air is bracing, the blood tingles in one's veins. Along an avenue of trees, the roads—which are good—with grades and curves enough to fascinate, soon lead to Beaver Lake, quiet, in the valleys. Then to the left that great mountain of jet black glass, Obsidian Cliff, looms up hundreds of feet high, and next Twin Lakes—one a lovely green, the other a somber black—two sisters, one in bridal garb, the other in deep mourning.

And just beyond a group of tents suggested that my appetite for things of earth had come back. A dinner for a dollar, and I got all I paid for; then out of the valley came smells of that other country that has been a standing menace to bad boys from time immemorial. Jets of steam rising in the air lead one down the road and suddenly you are in the midst of the grandest group of boiling springs in the world.

The smell is of the infernal regions. Spouting geysers of crystal water, boiling hot, boiling springs of purple, yellow and green waters are on every side. Awestruck with the mystery of the world, we moved along with hot water, smoke, steam, hissing noises and bad smells on every side.

Here, in the midst of Nature's grandest efforts, a storm broke loose, the rain fell, the lightning flashed, and thunder roared and crashed upon the mountainside, until the writer, who had found shelter under an overhanging rock, began to figure up his life insurance. Then the storm cleared away.

Having gone down hill several miles to cross Gibbon River, I began the climb again, mile after mile along winding hillsides, yet so gradual that very little walking was necessary; then along the summit of the mountain, with elk, antelope and deer in sight every few minutes; then down another long slope until the Madison River is reached; then for miles along an enchanted stream.

For miles the road leads through these marvels of the world until the Upper Geyser Basin is reached, and Old Faithful greets you with a spout of crystal water a hundred feet high. The giant roars a welcome. Almost countless boiling springs are on every side.

The road leads out through the pines, and a start is made for Yellowstone Lake sixteen miles away. Again the mountain road becomes too steep to ride, and we dismount and push our wheel up the winding hill until the summit is reached.

It is a perfect wheeling road that you traverse for miles after passing the divide. Then comes into view Yellowstone Lake, hid away in the midst of snow-capped mountains. The past fifteen miles has been through grand parks, along enchanting streams and meadows, and over roads lined with rarest wild flowers that fill the air with perfume.

A group of white tents on the bank of the lake, with the smell of roasting beef, broiling trout and coffee, calls one back to life. The wheel is set against a tree while a dinner is stowed away, and then rest on the grassy slopes in the balmy breezes that ruffle the green waters in the midst of God's grandest hills.

From this point there is a fine road for eighteen miles skirting the lake. Also, there is a small steamer that will convey you to the other side. Both ways are tempting and it is hard to decide, but sitting on the deck of a steamer is easier than sitting on a wheel. That settles it, and soon we are on the craft for a ride on waters that are magical with their green hues and shadows of the giant mountains.

It is 4 o'clock in the afternoon when a landing is made at the Lake Hotel, a tempting place to stop for the night. But in that latitude there are six hours of daylight still in which to make the seventeen miles to the Grand Canyon. The roads are fine and a start is made.

At Canyon Hotel a brook trout, hot from the broiler and as large as the platter, is set before one. A good dinner and a good bed followed the day, and the next day to come finds one still fascinated with the magnificence of the scene.

Another day, and the wheel is pushed three miles to the summit of the range. For three miles the road leads down the mountain past the Virginia Cascades, the road too rough to ride part of the way, then good wheeling except in a few places, back to Cinnabar, thirty-five miles.

In all, 172 miles had been made on the wheel, less about fifteen miles of walking up and down hill. Were there any mistakes? Yes, two of them. The wheel bucked one day and a header was taken down the hillside, and a bruised knee and torn trousers resulted, requiring the service of sticking plaster and a tailor.

Another time, the road being good and winding down hill around the base of a mountain, the wheel was fairly spinning along, when around a curve not twenty feet away was lying in the track a large black bear. There was every indication of a collision head-on, and the wheelman thought he would be telescoped. He yelled, then jumped, rolling over several times in the rose bushes, by the roadside. The wheel shot ahead. All this time the bear was "a humping of himself" to get out of the way. I don't know what he thought, but he went up the side of that mountain like a bounty jumper going to Canada. The wheel came out of the circus all right, but the rider had to take off his shoes to find his collar button.

— Abridged from C. E Belknap, "A Wheel Trip in Yellowstone Park." *League of American Wheelmen Bulletin and Good Roads* 24, no. 9 (August 28, 1896): 309–313.

Yellowstone's First Car

(1902)—Henry G. Merry

A man races his horseless carriage past waiting rangers and leads them on a merry chase.

Cars weren't officially admitted to Yellowstone Park until 1915, but that doesn't mean they weren't there before that. One story says that Henry G. Merry drove his Winton to Mammoth Hot Springs in 1902 to a dance at the National Hotel. He was caught—the story goes—but was allowed to drive out under cover of darkness. Here's a more colorful version told by his son.

When the Winton car arrived it was the conversation piece of the time. The word reached the commandant at the fort, along with the information that the noise it made was terrifying to horses. Very wisely he issued an order prohibiting this machine and others like if from the confines of Yellowstone Park. My father knew of this order, but thought he would pilot the car to the fort and talk things over with the commandant. In the interim, two troopers had been stationed at the entrance to prevent any such violation of the commandant's order.

As related in Father's diary, on June 2nd, 1902, he and my mother took off. When the north entrance was reached, he opened up the speed to about 25 mph, and the troopers' mounts acted up so that they could not block the passage. The machine was well on its way before they got their horses quieted down and started after the car—which was rapidly widening the distance between them.

All went well as long as the road was level but that was not for long. As the grade became steeper—the speed was reduced—and soon the car came to a stop. The troopers arrived at a hard gallop.

Fortunately, each one had a lariat and between the two horses they managed to pull the car to the commandant's office and gave him a report of how things happened. He was quite pleasant and took time to explain to father, who already knew, that the noise of his conveyance posed a threat to the lives of all tourists who were visiting the park in horse-drawn vehicles. Then he became quite stern and reminded him that he was still under arrest and would have to pay a penalty to be released. When my father asked what the penalty would be, the officer very seriously replied, "You will have to take me for a ride in this contraption." He got his ride and then assigned a detail to escort father to the gate.

— Text from the collection of the Pioneer Museum of Bozeman.

The Greatest Stagecoach Robbery

(1908)—Yellowstone Park Superintendent's Report

A lone gunman accosts seventeen coaches
and forces passengers to surrender their money
and jewelry, then escapes.

What was probably the greatest stagecoach robbery of the twentieth century in terms of people (174) and coaches (17) occurred in Yellowstone Park on August 24, 1908, but the bandit grossed only about two thousand dollars in cash and jewelry. The holdup man was never caught. A similar robbery of fourteen coaches occurred on July 29, 1914, but the holdup man was caught. Here's how the park superintendent described the events of 1908.

An unfortunate event, the hold-up of seventeen coaches, surreys, and spring wagons on the main road between Old Faithful Inn and the Thumb of Yellowstone Lake took place about 9 a.m. on August 24. The point was about four and a quarter miles from Old Faithful Inn on the road to the Thumb of Yellowstone Lake.

In accordance with the established time schedule, the first coach of Yellowstone Park Transportation Company loads at Old Faithful Inn at 7:30 o'clock in the morning; after all coaches of that company have been loaded, the Monida and Yellowstone Company coaches are loaded at the same point and follow after. These are followed in turn by the coaches of the Wylie Permanent Camping Company—all on the road eastward toward the Thumb.

This was the order of travel on the morning of August 24. As a precaution against dust and against accident on grades, drivers are instructed to maintain a distance of approximately 100 yards between coaches. On the morning in question eight vehicles were not molested by the robber.

It appears that the trooper on patrol passed the point where the robbery took place ahead of the first coaches. The interval between the eighth and ninth coaches in order of travel was rather extended, with an angle of the road intervening in a narrow defile, thickly wooded on either side.

The ninth vehicle was stopped by the robber with repeating rifle at "ready"; and in vulgar, blasphemous language he ordered a young man down from the box seat and made him carry a sack alongside the coach—into which passengers were commanded to deposit their money and jewelry. This was repeated with each of the sixteen vehicles following.

No one received physical injury excepting one passenger, whose actions did not suit the robber and who was disciplined by a stroke on the head with the gun, which was discharged at the same time. The injury was not reported serious.

Four of the looted coaches belonged to the Yellowstone Park Transportation Company, five to the Monida and Yellowstone Stage Company, and eight to the Wylie Permanent Camping Company. As near as can be learned by the separate memoranda handed in by the passengers the losses sustained by them in the robbery aggregated $1,363.95 cash and $730.25 in watches and jewelry. Upon being liberated the first coach of those robbed drove rapidly to the camp of the road sprinkling crew, located about 2 miles east of the hold-up point, where notice was given and a messenger dispatched to Old Faithful Inn—distant 6 miles—with news of the robbery.

The agent of the Yellowstone Park Transportation Company at the inn telegraphed the news to all stations in the park and notified the detail of soldiers stationed at Upper Geyser Basin, within a few hundred yards of the inn. He also states that he notified the officer in command of a troop of cavalry camped in the Lower Basin, about 9 miles distant by the old road. Telegraphic notice was received at Mammoth Hot Springs Hotel and immediately transmitted to my office by telephone. The message was repeated to Major Allen, who was up in the park, and he was requested to give the matter his personal attention.

All guard stations were warned and instructed and two scouts present at Mammoth were dispatched to the scene. They made the ride (49 miles) in four hours. Major Allen, who was in the park with General Edgerly, came into Mammoth the same evening, and on the following morning reported that he had given the necessary orders to his troops by telephone and telegraph from Norris.

The robber was on foot and disposed of a few pocketbooks and purses near the scene of the robbery, where they were found in a clump of bushes. One of these contained valuable papers and all were returned to their respective owners.

The trail could only be followed a short distance. The robber had apparently taken off his shoes and passed into a densely wooded region. All United States marshals, sheriffs, and peace officers in surrounding states, counties, and towns were duly notified and given description of the robber, as nearly as could be ascertained from tourists and drivers in the hold-up.

All passengers in their excitement blamed the soldiers. The character of the country is such that the entire Army of the United States could not prevent an evil-disposed man from entering the park with a gun.

On the date of the holdup one troop was on practice march in the park and was camped within 10 or 12 miles from Old Faithful Inn. One troop has been camped in Lower Geyser Basin all the season and one troop has been camped on Yellowstone River within a mile of Lake Hotel all the season.

So far it has been impossible to locate an escaped criminal who was convicted of poaching in the park and escaped from confinement in the military prison at Fort Yellowstone in October last. There seems to be a well-grounded suspicion that he is the perpetrator of this daring highway robbery. It is a slow and difficult task to conduct a systematic search for this criminal, without funds for expenses, by correspondence alone. The detectives in adjacent states, with whom I have corresponded since the robbery, work for a per diem and expenses and not for rewards offered, and although they have been informed that this office has no money for that purpose, they have never hesitated to give any information in their possession in regard to this particular matter.

— Report of the Superintendent of Yellowstone National Park. Yellowstone Park, Wyoming: Department of the Interior, October 15, 1908. 410-412.

Nights of Romance in Yellowstone Park

(1919)—R. Maury

*Pop Slocum takes a dive at a hot spring so
Winsted Tripp can meet the girl of his dreams.*

*Not all stories about Yellowstone Park are high adventures like fighting Indians or
tumbling down canyons or falling into geysers. Some are just sweet little tales about
falling in love. The author of this one doesn't say, but probably it's fiction. This fun
anecdote provides a sense of what visiting the park was like in the early 1900s.*

The giant Speedex hummed out of Bozeman with its load of khaki-clad,
riding-trousered women and men in old army uniforms. The running-board
was piled high with the dunnage that accompanies an automobile tour, and
in back, two burly, grey, spare tires rode majestic. The giant Speedex was
bound for Yellowstone Park.

Not two minutes behind roared Winsted Tripp's fiery roadster. The girl
was in the big machine ahead. In the hotel the night before, Win had noted
the entrance of the party; had heard the clerk describing the route they must
take to get to the park and had observed the girl. So it was that he had arisen
early, and was now sailing along with the top down and windshield up, the
breeze blowing over his thick hair and over the iron-grey ambrosial locks of
old Pop Slocum, who was accompanying him on his trip through the park.

All morning long the roadster sped down the Yellowstone Trail on its
way to the Gardiner gateway. Win kept a lookout for the Speedex, and twice
sighted the big spare tires down the dustless road ahead. He aimed to travel a
short distance behind the other party, and if necessary assist Fate in decreeing
that they should stop at the same hotel that night.

They made Mammoth Hot Springs about half-past four and secured a room. Then the young man with his old comrade went for a tour of the great hot springs formation. It was the cool of the afternoon, and the white lime-stone dust on the formation looked like snow. Old maids, college professors, geologists, guides, bored tourists, were everywhere, giving the multitudinous colored pools, spider web limestone deposits, and other wonders the great American "once-over."

Win thought once that he glimpsed the girl, but he couldn't be sure.

Those nights at Mammoth Hotel! The stars sparkling in the dry air of that high altitude; the arc lights flaring like giant diamonds around the grounds; the dance-floor in the hotel swimming in color as the couples sway to the orchestra's jangling tunes; the scent of balsam firs pervading every-thing in the park . . . Nights of romance!

"Go in and dance," urged Pop Slocum. "You may not know yon gay dam-sels, but tell 'em you're a gentleman and are taking as much risk as they are anyhow, and I'll bet no one will object."

But Win preferred to sit on the sidelines and watch the dancers. He had been a male wallflower since the first dance he had ever attended. He couldn't talk to girls, that was the trouble; he always felt called on to say something humorous or brilliant, and always managed to stammer out some peculiarly stupid remark.

And so, melancholy came upon Win, and he began to be afraid of his interest in the girl. She was too far above him, he concluded; she'd never understand. Finally, he went upstairs to bed.

The travelers went on early the next morning. They were getting into the heart of the great reserve, and the roads were becoming ever more tortuous and steep, though their ribbon-smooth surfacing continued.

Pop Slocum was surprised by Win's gloomy silence in the seat beside him. The old man had turned and stared for perhaps thirty seconds, while Win tried to look unconscious of it but felt the hot blood climbing to his ears.

"My God!" finally boomed the old man. "I might have known as much!"

"Known what?" asked Win.

"You're in love, my boy, in love! That's my diagnosis!"

Win grinned like a twelve-year-old boy.

"Correct you are, Pop," he admitted.

The Norris Geyser Basin rushed upon them around a curve, and Win drove his car off to the side of the road and stopped with a squall of brake linings. Below them was spread the basin, like the roof of hell's kitchen, smoking and steaming and hissing in a thousand vents.

The two men set out for the basin. They had walked hardly a dozen steps when the old man grasped Win's arm.

"There she is, lad!" he whispered, pointing towards the party out on the walk.

And there indeed she was, clad in an abbreviated yellow coat, khaki breeches, puttees, and battered old army hat. Win quickened his pace, and the old man giggled excitedly.

"Now, leave it to me, Bud," he instructed. "Just follow my lead, and keep wide awake."

They approached the party with all decent speed; the others had paused to examine a steam vent, and in no time, Win was able to get a satisfactory glance at the group. Pop Slocum was not idle. He had a way with him, which never gave offense yet admitted him to any company on terms of friendly and jovial intimacy. He had introduced himself and Win all around within three minutes.

And the girl? She smiled at Win frankly, as if she were meeting a friend again. She was about to say something, when Pop suddenly slipped and nearly tumbled into the hot water that lay on the thin crust of the basin. He grasped frantically and in so doing kicked the girl's foot so as to shove her towards Win.

She lost her balance, and fell into Win's arms. Perhaps he held her longer than was really necessary; at any rate he saw that she was thoroughly steady and in no danger of falling before letting her go. Pop had recovered, and the incident passed off. But Dorothy Brown's cheeks were bright with color; and Winsted Tripp was reduced to embarrassed silence.

＊＊＊

It was evening at the Grand Canyon Hotel. In the lobby the jazz band was putting "pep" into the couples weaving in and out on the polished floor. On the porch the older men smoked and talked of war and bolshevism and stock markets and automobiles, while the women gathered in those familiar gossip-circles, which they can never forego although they have the vote and sit in Congress.

A steep winding trail leads down from the Canyon Hotel to a platform overlooking the Lower Falls of the Yellowstone. Here Win had come, to sit in the moonlight and bid farewell to the romance he had possessed.

The night was bright with a full moon, and the canyon of the Yellowstone stretched away before him into infinity, a grey giant, dreaming under the stars. The roar of the river had become nearly soundless to Win's ears, its steady noise turning his nerves to its own pitch.

He was aroused from his reflections by the presence of someone else on the platform. He looked again, and rubbed his eyes.

"Oh, so it's you back again," he said confusedly.

"Yes," said Dorothy Brown, "It's I, back again."

Her tone had a little gladness that Win could not mistake. In that moment he knew his heart had found its objective.

— Condensed from R. Maury, "A Yellowstone Rencontre," *The University of Virginia Magazine* 63, no. 6 (October 1919): 221–232.

PART 8:
RAFTS, STEAMBOATS, AND STAIRWAYS

INTRODUCTION

Even after trains arrived and quality roads were built, going to see the sights remained a challenge.

By the end of the 1880s, a network of good roads allowed tourists to make a leisurely circuit of the major sights of Yellowstone Park in summer. But for the intrepid traveler, there were still adventures in the off-season and off the beaten path.

In winter, drifts of snow covered roads, and subzero temperatures kept visitors out. Finally, in 1887, an arctic explorer led a winter expedition into the park on "Norwegian snowshoes" (now called skis). The expedition was caught in a blizzard that sent temperatures down to minus thirty-seven degrees, but they discovered a whole new "Wonderland."

Even in summer some sights were accessible only by water. Travelers used rafts to cross the Yellowstone River so they could clamber down Uncle Tom's Trail to the base of the Lower Falls or view them from Artist Point. A cruise across Yellowstone Lake offered striking views and respite from dusty roads. And there was no adventure to beat whitewater rafting down Yankee Jim Canyon.

An Arctic Explorer Braves Yellowstone in Winter

(1887)—Jack Ellis Haynes

Travelers survive a blizzard at thirty-seven degrees below zero.

In the nineteenth century the very idea of winter travel in the park was so foreboding that the first winter trip there was led by an arctic explorer. Lieutenant Frederick Schwatka, who earned his fame exploring the frozen reaches of Alaska and Canada in 1878–80, led a group of a dozen men from Mammoth Springs to Norris Geyser Basin beginning on January 5, 1887. Schwatka fell ill at Norris, but Yellowstone photographer F. Jay Haynes and three others continued on to the Upper Geyser Basin and Yellowstone Falls. On their return trip they were stranded on Mount Washburn in a blinding snowstorm for seventy-two hours. Here's how F. Jay Haynes's son, Jack Ellis Haynes, told the story in 1920.

In January 1887, the first successful winter exploration of the Yellowstone region was made. Lieutenant Frederick Schwatka of Arctic fame headed the party consisting of several eastern men, F. Jay Haynes, photographer, and a corps of guides, packers and assistants. Their outfit consisted of astronomical instruments, photographic equipment, sleeping bags and provisions, which were drawn on toboggans; the party used Norwegian skis and Canadian web snowshoes, but the snow was so light that they sank readily and the toboggans were exceedingly difficult to draw. It took three days to cover the twenty miles from Mammoth Springs to Norris Basin; and the temperature the first night at Indian Creek was 37° below zero.

Yellowstone Park's sub-zero temperatures and deep snow kept travelers out until 1887, when an arctic explorer mounted an expedition. Here they are at Yancey's Hole in Pleasant Valley. NATIONAL PARK SERVICE

Unfortunately, Lieutenant Schwatka fell ill at Norris and was unable to proceed. Mr. Haynes, desirous of obtaining a collection of winter photographs of the park, employed two of the sturdiest men of the Schwatka party, and with Edward Wilson, a government scout, resumed the journey.

The toboggans were abandoned and this party packed their equipment and provisions on their backs—each man carrying about forty-five pounds.

Norris Basin was a gorgeous sight. Craters heretofore unnoticed by these men familiar with the park in summer, steamed conspicuously. The foliage was heavily laden with ice near the steam vents and geysers, producing all the fantastic forms possible to imagine, while the entire basin resembled a vast manufacturing center.

Tall trees buried in the snow appeared like bushes, and the general aspect of the country was completely changed, the average depth of the snow being about eight feet. The steam rising fully two thousand feet from the geysers at Upper Basin could be seen from the Lower Basin.

The beautifully colored walls of the Grand Canyon were masses of pure white. The north half of the Lower Falls hung in immense icicles 200 feet in length. An ice bridge fully 100 feet high was formed at the base of the falls, coming up to the spray line (about one-third the height of the falls). The brink was frozen over and was hidden in an arch of ice a dozen feet thick.

Thousands of elk were seen on the exposed ridges of Mount Washburn. The trip over Mount Washburn was one of most unusual hardship and privation; a blinding snowstorm, which lasted four days, overtook the party of four. During this entire time they wandered day and night without shelter, provisions or fire before reaching Yancey's ranch, an experience that nearly cost them their lives.

The circuit covered was about 200 miles, and the thermometer ranged from 10 to 50 degrees below zero during the twenty-nine days of the trip.

— From Jack Ellis Haynes, "Winter Exploration in 1887," *Haynes New Guide and Motorists' Complete Road Log of Yellowstone National Park* (J. E. Haynes: Saint Paul, 1920), 134–137.

Rafting across the Yellowstone to View the Canyon

(1896)—Burton Holmes

A travel writer rafts across the Yellowstone River to view the falls from Artist Point.

In 1896 famous lecturer, filmmaker, and writer Burton Holmes visited Yellowstone Park. Holmes, who coined the word travelogues, *wrote about his Yellowstone trip in Volume 6 of his ten-volume series by that name.*

After describing the Grand Canyon of the Yellowstone from several vantage points on the north rim, Holmes told this story about crossing the Yellowstone River on a crude raft made of logs to see the Lower Falls from Artist Point.

Most travelers are content to view the canyon from the points to which I have already led you. Others remain unsatisfied until they have looked into the great chasm from "Artists' Point," the one perfect point of view, which is unfortunately on the other bank, and in 1896 was well nigh inaccessible.

There was no bridge; the crossing of the river below the falls was utterly out of the question; but there remained the possibility of crossing far above the upper gorge, where the waters, although swift-flowing, present a level, navigable surface. But there has not been a boat upon the river since the last one, very fortunately empty, was swept away and dashed to pieces by the cataracts. No boat! No bridge!

The river being now too deep and swift to ford, I turn in my difficulty to the gallant soldiers of Uncle Sam, who are stationed at the canyon. The sergeant in command at the little military camp enthusiastically comes to my assistance, and at sunrise next morning I find him a little way above the rapids, slowly poling upstream a raft, which he has built expressly for our excursion.

At last, we reach a point from which he deems it safe to put out into the current, where the waters, swift as those of a millrace, are gliding on in their eagerness to plunge into the yawning canyon, just one mile beyond. There was, of course, no actual danger, yet the thought was ever present that our raft, if left to its own devices, would at once follow unresistingly that treacherous flood, bound through the rapids and plunge over the first fall, then dash through the upper canyon, and finally meet annihilation in the whirlpools at the bottom of the great cataract.

In safety, however, we arrive on the farther shore. Then we skirt the right bank through a thick growth of pine, and while we are walking through the forest, thundershowers come and go with great frequency and fury. We are soon drenched to the skin, but pressing on we reach the edge of the forest; the earth appears to open at our feet, and the canyon yawns before us, deep and mysterious. Vapors are surging upward from its depths, but fortunately, the sun is beginning to break through the clouds above.

A shaft of sunshine touches a portion of the opposing wall, and another brilliantly illuminates the pinnacles of white and gold, while others chase the vapors rapidly away. The fears that rain and fog will render our excursion fruitless are dispelled, as, reaching another point of view, we exchange salutes with friends on the other rim.

We shout to them, they shout to us; but the sounds meet only halfway and then fall into the depths between. We cannot hear, nor are we ourselves heard. The river's rumbling mocks our puny efforts to span the deep chasm with a bridge of vocal sound. We must attempt to span it with our gaze.

Few of the great sights of this world have power to thrill us more than this vista of the canyon of the Yellowstone. We are unable to tell what most impresses us: the immensity of the great gulf, the infinite glory of its colored walls, the struggling river far below, the stately army of tall pines massed on the brink and pressing forward, apparently as eager as we to drink in all the splendor of the scene.

All these things go to compose the scene, to form that indefinable majesty that inspires us—to hold our peace. Silence is the only eloquence that can avail us here. No man has yet found language to express the majesty of this abyss of color. But, we ask, will no voice ever perfectly express in words what we all feel but dare not, cannot speak? Will no great poet of the new world, inspired by these grandeurs, ever utter the immortal song in which our vaguest thoughts shall find interpretation? Great, great indeed must be the soul of him who would give adequate expression to the reverential awe inspired by a scene like this.

But what is man that he should strive to utter the unutterable? The emotions that overwhelm us here can be expressed only in one language, and that is not a mortal language; it is the language of those to whom all mysteries have been revealed—the great eternal, wordless language of the soul: a language that we may not understand until the gates of death have closed behind us.

— From *Burton Holmes Travelogues,* Volume 6 (The McClure Company: New York, 1905), 104–112.

Crashing through Yankee Jim Canyon

(c. 1902)—Lewis Ransome Freeman

An adventurer tries to impress a girl while guiding a wooden raft through Yankee Jim Canyon.

Today it's easy to hire a boat with a guide to run the rapids through Yankee Jim Canyon north of Yellowstone Park. But that wasn't always the case, as Lewis Ransome Freeman discovered more than a hundred years ago.

After graduating from Stanford University in 1898, Freeman decided to become an adventurer and traveled America, Asia, Africa, and the Pacific Islands. About 1902, after snowshoeing through Yellowstone Park, he decided to float to the Gulf of Mexico down the Yellowstone, Missouri, and Mississippi Rivers. His first obstacle was to get through Yankee Jim Canyon, a rugged stretch of the Yellowstone River just north of the park.

Freeman solicited help from Yankee Jim George, a colorful character who had lived for thirty years in the canyon that bears his name. The government had taken over Jim's toll road by then, but he still provided accommodations in his rustic cabin. And, he knew where Freeman could get a boat.

Freeman covered the Russo-Japanese War beginning in 1905 and continued to work as a war correspondent through World War I. It wasn't until 1922 that he published this description of running the rapids of Yankee Jim Canyon.

The boat I secured about ten miles down river from the park boundary. The famous "Yankee Jim" gave it to me. This may sound generous on Jim's part, but seeing the boat didn't belong to him it wasn't especially so. Nor was the craft really a boat.

We found the craft where it had been abandoned at the edge of an eddy. It was high and dry on the rocks. Plain as it was that neither boat-builder nor even carpenter had had a hand in its construction, there was still no possible doubt of its tremendous strength and capacity to withstand punishment.

Jim said that a homesick miner had built this fearful and wonderful craft with the idea of using it to return to his family in Hickman, Kentucky. He had bade defiance to the rapids of the Yellowstone with the slogan "HICK-MAN OR BUST." Kentucky Mule he had called it.

Our plan of operation was something like this: Bill and Herb, the neighboring ranchers, were to go up and help me push off, while Jim went down to the first fall at the head of the canyon to be on hand to pilot me through. If I made the first riffle all right, I was to try to hold up the boat in an eddy until Jim could amble down to the second fall and stand-by to signal me my course into that one in turn, and so on down through.

I was to take nothing with me save my camera. My bags were to remain in Jim's cabin until he had seen me pass from sight below the canyon. Then he was to send the stuff on to me at Livingston.

As I swung round the bend above the head of the canyon, I espied old Jim awaiting my coming on a rocky vantage above the fall. A girl in a gingham gown had dismounted from a calico pony and was climbing up to join us. With fore-blown hair and skirt, she cut an entrancing silhouette against the sun-shot morning sky.

I think the presence of that girl had a deal to do with the impending disaster, for I would never have thought of showing off if none but Jim had been there. But something told me that the exquisite creature could not but admire the sangfroid of a youth who would let his boat drift while he stood up and took a picture of the thundering cataract over which it was about to plunge.

And so I did it—just that. Then, waving my camera above my head to attract Jim's attention to the act, I tossed it ashore. That was about the only sensible thing I did in my run through the canyon.

As I resumed my steering oar, I saw that Jim was gesticulating wildly in an apparent endeavor to attract my attention to a comparatively rock-free chute down the left bank. Possibly if I had not wasted valuable time displaying my sangfroid I might have worried the Mule over in that direction, and headed right for a clean run through.

As it was, the contrary brute simply took the bit in her teeth and went waltzing straight for the reef of barely submerged rock at the head of the steeply cascading pitch of white water. Broadside on she sunk into the hollow of a refluent wave, struck crashingly fore and aft, and hung trembling while the full force of the current of the Yellowstone surged against her upstream gunwale.

Looking back up-stream as the reeling Mule swung in the current, I saw Jim, with the Gingham Girl in his wake, ambling down the bank at a broken-kneed trot in an apparent endeavor to head me to the next fall as per schedule.

Poor old chap! He was never a hundred-to-one shot in that race now that the Mule had regained her head and was running away down mid-channel regardless of obstacles. He stumbled and went down even as I watched him with the tail of my eye. The Gingham Girl pulled him to his feet and he seemed to be leaning heavily against her fine shoulder as the Mule whisked me out of sight around the next bend.

With the steering oar permanently unshipped there was more difficulty than ever in exercising any control over the balkiness of the stubborn Mule. After a few ineffectual attempts, I gave up trying to do anything with the oar and confined my navigation to fending off with a cottonwood pike-pole.

This really helped no more than the oar, so it was rather by good luck than anything else that the Mule hit the next pitch head on and galloped down it with considerable smartness. When she reeled through another rapid beam-on without shipping more than a bucket or two of green water I concluded she was quite able to take care of herself, and so sat down to enjoy the scenery.

I was still lounging at ease when we came to a sharp right-angling notch of a bend where the full force of the current was exerted to push a sheer wall of red-brown cliff out of the way. Not unnaturally, the Mule tried to do the same thing. That was where I discovered I had over-rated her strength of construction.

I have said that she impressed me at first sight as being quite capable of nosing the Rock of Gibraltar out of her way. This optimistic estimate was not borne out. That little patch of cliff was not high enough to make a respectable footstool for the guardian of the Mediterranean, but it must have been quite as firmly socketed in the earth. So far as I could see it budged never the breadth of a hair when the Mule, driving at all of fifteen miles an hour, crashed into it with the shattering force of a battering ram. Indeed, everything considered, it speaks a lot for her construction that she simply telescoped instead of resolving into cosmic stardust. Even the telescoping was not quite complete.

The Mule had ceased to be a boat and become a raft, but not a raft constructed on scientific principles. The one most desirable characteristic of a properly built raft of logs is its stability. It is almost impossible to upset. The remains of the Mule had about as much stability as a toe dancer, and all of the capriciousness.

She kept more or less right side up on to the head of the next riffle and then laid down and negotiated the undulating waves by rolling. I myself, after she had spilled me out at the head of the riffle, rode through on one of her planks, but it was a railroad tie, with a big spike in it, that rasped me over the ear in the whirlpool at the foot.

And so I went on through to the foot of Yankee Jim Canyon. In the smoother water, I clung to a tie, plank or the thinning remnants of the Mule herself. At the riffles, to avoid another clout on the head from the spike-fanged flotsam, I found it best to swim ahead and flounder through on my own. I was not in serious trouble at any time, for much the worst of the rapids had been those at the head of the canyon. Had I been really hard put for it, there were a dozen places at which I could have crawled out. As that would have made overtaking the Mule again somewhat problematical, I was reluctant to do it. Also, no doubt, I was influenced by the fear that Jim and the Gingham Girl might call me a quitter.

Beaching what I must still call the Mule on a bar where the river fanned out in the open valley at the foot of the canyon, I dragged her around into an eddy and finally moored her mangled remains to a friendly cottonwood on the left bank. Taking stock of damages, I found that my own scratches and bruises, like Beauty, were hardly more than skin deep. As the day was bright and warm and the water not especially cold, I decided to make way while the sun shone—to push on toward Livingston.

The rest of that day's run was more a matter of chills than thrills, especially after the evening shadows began to lengthen and the northerly wind to strengthen. The Mule repeated her roll-and-reduce tactics every time she came to a stretch of white water.

There were only three planks left when I abandoned her at dusk, something over twenty miles from the foot of the canyon, and each of these was sprinkled as thickly with spike-points as a Hindu fakir's bed of nails. One plank, by a curious coincidence, was the strake that had originally borne the defiant slogan, "HICKMAN OR BUST." Prying it loose from its cumbering mates, I shoved it gently out into the current.

Spending the night with a hospitable rancher, I walked into Livingston in the morning. There I found my bags and camera, which good old "Yankee Jim" had punctually forwarded by the train.

— Condensed from Lewis Ransome Freeman, *Down the Yellowstone* (New York: Dodd, Mead and Company, 1922), Introduction and pages 65-76.

Cruising Yellowstone Lake

(1903)—Hester Ferguson Henshall

*The wife of a fish biologist cruises
Yellowstone Lake, admiring the scenery and
watching an angry bison on Dot Island.*

*Hester Henshall traveled by train from Bozeman to Yellowstone Park in 1903
with her husband Dr. James Henshall, who was director of the federal fish hatchery
in Bozeman. Dr. Henshall was a physician, but he made his name as an angler
and fish biologist. His* Book of the Black Bass, *published in 1881, is still prized
by anglers.*

*The Henshalls toured Yellowstone "the Wylie Way," that is, with Wylie Per-
manent Camping Company, which offered tourists a comprehensive package that
included transportation, food, and lodging in tents that were put up in the spring
and left up for the season. The tour included a steamboat cruise across Yellowstone
Lake. Here's Hester's description of that.*

The shrill whistle of the little steamer called us aboard. She is a steel boat,
with her name "Zillah" on a white flag floating at her masthead. We were
soon steaming out into the lake. The captain's name was Waters, a good name
for a steamboat captain. Miss Lillian Ehlert was soon at the wheel steering
under the care of the pilot.

Doctor Henshall and Doctor Donaldson and myself sat in the bow of
the boat. The scene was beautiful and was all very fascinating to me. Upon
the mountains was a vague blue efflorescent haze like the bloom upon a
grape, that made the tint deeper, richer, softer, whether it were the deep blue
of the farthest reach of vision, or the somber gray of the nearer mountains, or
the densely verdant slopes of the foot-hills that dipped down into the dark
shadowy waters of the lake.

Along the eastern shore was the Absaroka Range of mountains; and in one place was seen the profile of a human face, formed by two peaks of the lofty range. The face is upturned toward the sky and is known as the Giant's Face. It was several minutes before I recognized the resemblance, and then I wondered at my stupidity.

We stopped at Dot Island, a tiny green isle in the middle of the lake, on which are a number of animals, buffalo, elk, deer and antelope. They were fed with hay from the steamboat while we were there. The captain warned us not to go near, as the big bull buffalo was very fierce. He finally did make a terrific rush and butted the fence until I feared the structure would go down before his fierce onslaughts. He was the last animal fed, and the doctor said that was the cause of his demonstration; that it was all for effect, and to get us aboard again as the captain wanted to get the passengers to land at his curio store in season. The man brought another bale of hay and fed the big buffalo, who suddenly became very docile, and we left him quietly munching his hay. I guess the doctor was right.

Soon we were again steaming over the lake. We three again took our places at the bow, and thought it queer that others did not want them. We were told that the "Zillah" was brought from Lake Minnetonka, Minnesota, in sections and put together at the lake, which seemed wonderful to me, as she had a steel hull. Too soon our journey was at an end.

— From Hester Ferguson Henshall's journal, *A Trip Through Yellowstone National Park* (1903), Montana Historical Society Archives.

At the dawn of the twentieth century, steamship Zillah *gave travelers respite from dusty roads and a scenic cruise across Lake Yellowstone.* NATIONAL PARK SERVICE

Skiing with Theodore Roosevelt in Yellowstone Park

(1903)—John Burroughs

A famous naturalist watches the president flounder on skis.

In 1903 President Theodore Roosevelt invited John Burroughs to join him on a two-week trip to Yellowstone National Park. At the time, Burroughs was a very popular writer whose nature essays were compared to those of Henry David Thoreau.

Roosevelt and Burroughs had built a long-term friendship on their mutual respect and love of nature. They corresponded regularly, mostly about natural history. The president called Burroughs "Oom John" because of his flowing white whiskers.

The pair crossed the country in Roosevelt's private Pullman car, stopping at cities and towns where the president met local dignitaries and gave speeches. Between cities the president reminisced about his life as a rancher and sportsman.

When they reached the entrance of the park at Gardiner, Roosevelt left reporters and his secret service guards behind and went through the park accompanied only by Burroughs, Park Superintendent John Pitcher, and a small entourage.

The sixty-five-year-old Burroughs was afraid he wouldn't be able the keep up with the forty-four-year-old president, who had a larger-than-life reputation for physical stamina. Here's Burroughs's description of what happened when the pair went skiing.

At the Canyon Hotel the snow was very deep, and had become so soft from the warmth of the earth beneath, as well as from the sun above, that we could only reach the brink of the canyon on skis. The president and Major Pitcher had used skis before, but I had not, and, starting out without the customary pole, I soon came to grief. The snow gave way beneath me, and I was soon in an awkward predicament. The more I struggled, the lower my head and

President Theodore Roosevelt visited Yellowstone Park many times. While in office in 1903 he took a winter trip there with naturalist John Burroughs (right).
NATIONAL PARK SERVICE

shoulders went, till only my heels, strapped to those long timbers, protruded above the snow. To reverse my position was impossible till some one came, and reached me the end of a pole, and pulled me upright. But I very soon got the hang of the things, and the president and I quickly left the superintendent behind. I think I could have passed the president, but my manners forbade. He was heavier than I was, and broke in more. When one of his feet would go down half a yard or more, I noted with admiration the skilled diplomacy he displayed in extricating it. The tendency of my skis was all the time to diverge, and each to go off at an acute angle to my main course, and I had constantly to be on the alert to check this tendency.

Paths had been shoveled for us along the brink of the canyon, so that we got the usual views from the different points. The canyon was nearly free from snow, and was a grand spectacle, by far the grandest to be seen in the park. The president told us that once, when pressed for meat, while returning through here from one of his hunting trips, he had made his way down to the river that we saw rushing along beneath us, and had caught some trout for dinner. Necessity alone could induce him to fish.

Across the head of the falls there was a bridge of snow and ice, upon which we were told that the coyotes passed. As the season progressed, there would come a day when the bridge would not be safe. It would be interesting to know if the coyotes knew when this time arrived.

The only live thing we saw in the canyon was an osprey perched upon a rock opposite us.

Near the falls of the Yellowstone, as at other places we had visited, a squad of soldiers had their winter quarters. The president always called on them, looked over the books they had to read, examined their housekeeping arrangements, and conversed freely with them.

In front of the hotel were some low hills separated by gentle valleys. At the president's suggestion, he and I raced on our skis down those inclines. We had only to stand up straight, and let gravity do the rest. As we were going swiftly down the side of one of the hills, I saw out of the corner of my eye the president taking a header into the snow. The snow had given way beneath him, and nothing could save him from taking the plunge. I don't know whether I called out, or only thought, something about the downfall of the administration. At any rate, the administration was down, and pretty well buried, but it was quickly on its feet again, shaking off the snow with a boy's laughter. I kept straight on, and very soon the laugh was on me, for the treacherous snow sank beneath me, and I took a header, too.

"Who is laughing now, Oom John?" called out the president.

The spirit of the boy was in the air that day about the Canyon of the Yellowstone, and the biggest boy of us all was President Roosevelt.

— Excerpt from John Burroughs, "Camping with the President," *Atlantic Monthly* 67 (May 1906): 585–600.

A Near Tragedy
on Uncle Tom's Trail

(1911)—Louis Downing

A young woman almost tumbles down
Yellowstone Canyon while her friends scramble
to the base of the Lower Falls.

When Louis Downing visited Yellowstone National Park in 1911, good roads, comfortable hotels and camps, and tour guides left little room for adventure. But, as Downing found out, travelers could still get a thrill by taking "Uncle Tom's Trail" to the base of the Lower Falls.

Downing, a druggist from Hamilton, Montana, toured the park "the Wylie Way," with a group of people he called "the family," because they had become such fine friends on the trip. Here's his description of what happened to members of the family when they decided to descend "Uncle Tom's Trail."

After sending a few cards, Grace D., Mr. Jewell, Jane D., Sis, Lee and Doc followed a pretty trail through the forest to Uncle Tom's Trail. A big sign marked "Dangerous" hung at the top.

At the bottom of the trail, we could see a guide helping two women down—almost lifting them from rock to rock. Jane D. promptly decided that long skirts and high heels were not safe on that trail and refused to start. The boys agreed with her, but Grace, who wore flat heels, had started.

Sis wanted to go but agreed to remain at the top with Jane D. Doc went down like a squirrel. Mr. Jewell and Lee remained near Grace. Almost half way down Brother Lee's Kodak fell to the bottom and broke into a dozen pieces. When they reached the river, they sat on a large rock and drank some of the water. They were directly under the fall, and the view in either direction was magnificent.

A light rain caused them to fear that the slippery rocks would make ascent dangerous so they started up the trail though they could have spent hours in the canyon. They reached the top in twenty-two minutes.

Following the roadway, they came to a flight of stairs leading to a platform built close to the fall. The green water and white foam plunging over the rocks was simply magnificent.

Grace D. says the climb up those steps was the hardest she had ever taken; yet, the view was worth the effort. Doc took a picture of the fall from this point.

In the meantime, the girls sat at the top of the trail—the mosquitoes swarming about them. They had almost made up their minds to start down when Sis slipped and fell a little to the left of the trail. She slid several feet before she could get hold of a rock that would hold her. Even then she realized that it would soon loosen, so while Jane D. frantically shouted for help Sis managed to pull herself up to the roots of a tree while the mosquitoes settled on her arms making it almost impossible to hold on.

Jane D. tried to signal the boys, but they were too far away to realize what she meant and merely waved their hands. She knew that Sis could not hold on much longer, so she ran toward the road and finally attracted the attention of several tourists. Mr. L. F. Huesselmann of Osage, Iowa, reached the scene first, but Sis, knowing that he could not pull her up alone, held on until Mr. W. F. Schroeder of Oakland, California, reached the trail. They succeeded in getting her up and several feet from the trail before she weakened and sat down. Jane D. was pale and nervous and Mrs. Schroeder was badly frightened. She said her knees had just given way when she saw Sis hanging above the trail.

Sis herself was over the fright in a few minutes, and laughed hysterically, but poor Jane D. couldn't see anything to laugh at and said so.

— From the diary of Louis E. Downing, which is in the K. Ross Toole Archives, Mansfield Library, University of Montana, Missoula.

PART 9:
HUNTING

INTRODUCTION

Early hunters decimated big game in Yellowstone Park, but army rangers brought it back.

The law that established Yellowstone Park in 1872 explicitly made hunting in the park legal. The rationale was that visitors to the remote wilderness would need to kill animals for food, but people took the law for general permission to hunt. In fact the abundance of big game was a prime attraction for early tourists. Trophy hunters sought specimens of the magnificent deer, elk, moose, and bison that lived in the pristine wilderness. Additionally commercial hunters, who had wiped out the enormous buffalo herds of the Great Plains, shot elk by the thousands to supply hides to leather manufacturers.

By the 1880s hunters had decimated the once-abundant game herds. The secretary of the interior promulgated regulations banning hunting in 1883, but the slaughter continued, because officials didn't have any way to stop it. In fact one of the primary reasons the army took over administration of the park in 1886 was to end the wildlife holocaust.

The army forced visitors to leave their guns behind or have them sealed at the park boundary, but demand for trophy buffalo heads and decorative elk teeth continued to attract poachers. Also, the regulations were interpreted to exempt predators like wolves and mountain lions in the mistaken belief that killing them would help ungulates. Although hunting is still prohibited in the park, hunters still flock to the surrounding areas to harvest trophy animals that leave its protective borders.

Wapiti Are the Stupidest Brutes

(1874)—The Earl of Dunraven

"There was a fine stag in the herd, but he managed to get himself well among the hinds out of harm's way."

Windham Thomas Wyndam-Quin, the fourth earl of Dunraven, mounted a hunting expedition of Yellowstone Park in 1874. Lord Dunraven hired several men to accompany him. One of them was Fredrick Bottler, a rancher who settled in the Paradise Valley on the Yellowstone River in the 1860s. Bottler was familiar with Yellowstone's wonders and served as an outfitter, guide, and hunter for several early expeditions.

Dunraven, who had been a war correspondent for British newspapers, was an astute observer with a droll wit. He wrote several books about his travel adventures. Here's his description of elk hunting in Yellowstone Park.

We wound our way towards the head of the valley, half asleep, for the day was very hot. Before long I jerked my horse on to his haunches and slid quietly off. The others followed my example without a word, for they too had caught a glimpse of the dark brown forms of some wapiti feeding quietly in the wood. Bottler, in his enthusiasm, seized me violently by the arm and hurried into the timber, ejaculating at every glimpse of the forms moving through the trees.

"There they go! There they go! Shoot! Now then! There's a chance." At the time he was dragging me along, and I could no more shoot than fly. At last I shook myself clear of him, and, getting a fair easy shot at a large fat doe, fired and killed her.

Wapiti are the stupidest brutes in creation; and, instead of making off at once, the others all bunched up and stared about them, so that we got two more before they made up their minds to clear out. There was a fine stag in the herd, but, as is usually the case, he managed to get himself well among the hinds out of harm's way, and none of us could get a chance at him.

Magnificent animals drew sportsmen to Yellowstone Park until the army forbade hunting in 1886. After that, hunters continued to bag magnificent trophies like this six-point elk shot in Jackson Hole in 1889. GALLATIN HISTORY MUSEUM

Bottler and I followed his tracks for an hour, but could not come up with him; and, finding that he had taken clear up the mountain, we returned to the scene of action. There we found the rest of the party busily engaged in cutting up the huge deer. One of them was a hind, in first-rate condition and as fat as butter. We were very glad of fresh meat, and, as the ground was very suitable, determined to camp right there, and send some of the flesh down to the main camp in the morning. We pitched our Lilliputian tents at the foot of one of a hundred huge hemlocks, set a fire, and proceeded to make ourselves comfortable for the night.

We were all smoking round the fire—a most attentive audience, watching with much interest the culinary feats which Bottler was performing—when we were startled by a most unearthly sound.

Bottler knew it well, but none of us strangers had ever heard a wapiti stag roaring before, and it is no wonder we were astonished at the noise. The wapiti bellows forth one great roar, commencing with a hollow, harsh, unnatural sound, and ending in a shrill screech like the whistle of a locomotive.

In about ten minutes this fellow called again, a good deal nearer, and the third time he was evidently close to camp, so we started out. Advancing cautiously, we presently, through a bush, distinguished in the gloom then I saw body and antlered head of a real monarch of the forest as he stalked out into an open glade and stared with astonishment at our fire.

He looked perfectly magnificent. He was a splendid beast, and his huge bulk, looming large in the uncertain twilight, appeared gigantic. He stood without betraying the slightest sign of fear or hesitation; but, as if searching with proud disdain for the intruder that had dared to invade his solitude, he slowly swept round the branching spread of his antlers, his neck extended and his head a little thrown back, and snuffed the air.

I could not see the fore sight of the little muzzle-loader, but luck attended the aim, for the bullet struck high up the shoulder; and, shot through the spine, the largest wapiti stag that I had ever killed fell stone-dead in his tracks.

It was early in the season, and his hide was in first rate condition, a rich glossy brown on the sides and jet black along the back and on the legs; so we turned to, cut off his head and skinned him; and, by the time we had done that and had packed the head and hide into camp, it was pitch dark, when we were ready for supper and blankets.

— From the Earl of Dunraven, "Wapiti and Grizzlies," *Hunting in the Yellowstone,* Horace Kephart, ed. (New York: Outing Publishing Company, 1917), 130–160.

The Antelope That Got Away

(1874)—The Earl of Dunraven

A downed buck springs to life and terrifies a hunter.

While returning from Yellowstone Park in 1874, the Earl of Dunraven discovered he was running out of "grub." Hunting for food in the park was legal then, so he decided to replenish the larder by bagging an antelope. He went hunting with pioneer rancher and Yellowstone guide Fred Bottler and a helper named Wynne.

While the trio was pursuing a large buck, a ferocious hailstorm forced them to take cover under a pine tree. When the storm abated, Dunraven spotted the buck, tried a long shot, and missed. Here's his story of what happened after that.

It was blowing so hard, and there was such a noise of storm, that there was no danger of the shot having disturbed anything, and so, as the country looked very gamey, we walked on, leading the horses. Presently we came upon a little band containing six antelopes.

We were by this time near the summit of a long sloping mountain. The ground fell away rapidly on either side, and in a long but narrow glade the antelopes were lying. While we were peering at them, two does—nasty inquisitive females—got up, walked forward a few steps and stared too. We remained still as statues, and after a while they appeared satisfied and began to crop the grass. We then left our ponies, and signing to Wynne, who just then hove in sight, that there was something ahead, and that he was to catch them, hastened up under cover of some brush.

By the time we reached the tree nearest to them we found the does had all got up and fled to some distance, but a splendid buck with a very large pair of horns was still lying down. At him I fired, and nailed him. He gave one spring straight into the air from his bed, fell back into the same spot, kicked once or twice convulsively, and lay still. I fired the second barrel at a doe and struck her, for she "pecked" almost on to her head, but she recovered and went on.

Out we rushed: "Never mind the dead one," shouts Bottler, his face all aglow; "let's get the other; she's twice as good, and can't go far. You take one side of that clump and I will take the other." So off we set, best pace, bursting up the hill after the wounded doe. We followed her for half an hour, running our level best, and got each a long shot, but missed; and, as she was evidently quite strong, we gave up the chase and walked back.

We found Wynne driving up the ponies. He appeared to have some little trouble with the poor beasts, which were rendered sulky and ill tempered by the wet and cold, so I said to Bottler, "You go down and help him, and I will butcher the buck."

I had scarcely got the words "butcher the buck" out of my mouth, when the darned thing, apparently not appreciating my intentions, came to life, bounded to his feet, sprang into the air, coming down all four feet together, and, with his legs widely extended, gave a phwit—a sort of half whistle, half snort of surprise, I suppose at his own resurrection—stared a second, and made off.

"Shoot, Bottler," I cried, "shoot. In heaven's name, man, can't you see the buck?" and I threw up my own rifle and missed him of course. "By George," says Bottler, wheeling round, "look at the ___;" and he let go at him with the same result.

Wynne yelled and dropped the lariats; Bottler ejaculated terrible things; and I also, I fear, made use of very cursory remarks. But neither for swearing, shouting, nor shooting would he stop. He ran about fifty yards, fell on his head and rolled over and over, jumped up again, ran one hundred yards, pitched head over heels the second time, got up, and went down the hill as if he had never felt better in his life.

We followed of course, and wasted an hour in searching for him in vain. Never again will I pass a beast, however dead he may appear to be, without cutting his throat by way of making sure.

— From the Earl of Dunraven, "Tracking Back," *Hunting in the Yellowstone*, Horace Kephart, ed., (New York: Outing Publishing Company, 1917), 288–313.

TR Seeks the Thrill of Killing Endangered Bison

(1889)—Theodore Roosevelt

The future president stalks the last of a dying species and kills it.

American bison once numbered thirty million or more, but by the middle of the 1880s, commercial hunters had decimated the herds that once darkened the prairies. But the fact that the bison was nearing extinction didn't deter sportsmen from pursuing the thrill of killing one of the magnificent animals.

Even Theodore Roosevelt, who is renowned for his role in the American conservation movement and environment preservation, could not resist the temptation of bison hunting. Here's how he described the experience.

In the fall of 1889, I heard that a very few bison were still left around the head of Wisdom River. Thither I went and hunted faithfully; there was plenty of game of other kind, but of bison not a trace did we see. Nevertheless a few days later that same year I came across these great wild cattle at a time when I had no idea of seeing them.

We had gone out to find moose, but had seen no sign of them, and had then begun to climb over the higher peaks with an idea of getting sheep. The old hunter who was with me was, very fortunately, suffering from rheumatism, and he therefore carried a long staff instead of his rifle; I say fortunately, for if he had carried his rifle it would have been impossible to stop his firing at such game as bison, nor would he have spared the cows and calves.

About the middle of the afternoon we crossed a low, rocky ridge, above timberline, and saw at our feet a basin or round valley of singular beauty. The ground rose in a pass evidently much frequented by game in bygone days, their trails lying along it in thick zigzags, each gradually fading out after a few hundred yards, and then starting again in a little different place, as game trails so often seem to do.

We bent our steps toward these trails, and no sooner had we reached the first than the old hunter bent over it with a sharp exclamation of wonder. There in the dust were the unmistakable hoof-marks of a small band of bison, apparently but a few hours old. There had been half a dozen animals in the party, one a big bull and two calves.

We immediately turned and followed the trail. It led down to the little lake, where the beasts had spread and grazed on the tender, green blades, and had drunk their fill. The footprints then came together again, showing where the animals had gathered and walked off in single file to the forest.

It was a very still day, and there were nearly three hours of daylight left. Without a word my silent companion, who had been scanning the whole country with hawk-eyed eagerness, besides scrutinizing the sign on his hands and knees, took the trail, motioning me to follow. In a moment we entered the woods, breathing a sigh of relief as we did so; for while in the meadow we could never tell that the buffalo might not see us, if they happened to be lying in some place with a commanding lookout.

The old hunter was thoroughly roused, and he showed himself a very skillful tracker. We were much favored by the character of the forest, which was rather open, and in most places free from undergrowth and down timber. The ground was covered with pine needles and soft moss, so that it was not difficult to walk noiselessly. Once or twice when I trod on a small dry twig, or let the nails in my shoes clink slightly against a stone, the hunter turned to me with a frown of angry impatience; but as he walked slowly, continually halting to look ahead, as well as stooping over to examine the trail, I did not find it very difficult to move silently.

At last, we saw a movement among the young trees not fifty yards away. Peering through the safe shelter yielded by some thick evergreen bushes, we speedily made out three bison, a cow, a calf, and a yearling. Soon another cow and calf stepped out after them. I did not wish to shoot, waiting for the appearance of the big bull, which I knew was accompanying them.

So for several minutes I watched the great, clumsy, shaggy beasts, as all unconscious they grazed in the open glade. Mixed with the eager excitement of the hunter was a certain half melancholy feeling as I gazed on these bison, themselves part of the last remnant of a doomed and nearly vanished race.

Few, indeed, are the men who now have, or ever more shall have, the chance of seeing the mightiest of American beasts, in all his wild vigor, surrounded by the tremendous desolation of his far-off mountain home.

At last, when I had begun to grow very anxious lest the others should take alarm, the bull likewise appeared on the edge of the glade, and stood with outstretched head, scratching his throat against a young tree, which shook violently. I aimed low, behind his shoulder, and pulled trigger. At the crack of the rifle all the bison, without the momentary halt of terror-struck surprise so common among game, turned and raced off at headlong speed.

The fringe of young pines beyond and below the glade cracked and swayed as if a whirlwind were passing, and in another moment they reached the top of a very steep incline, thickly strewn with boulders and dead timber. Down this they plunged with reckless speed; their surefootedness was a marvel in such seemingly unwieldy beasts. A column of dust obscured their passage, and under its cover they disappeared in the forest; but the trail of the bull was marked by splashes of frothy blood, and we followed it at a trot.

Fifty yards beyond the border of the forest we found the stark black body stretched motionless. He was a splendid old bull, still in his full vigor, with large, sharp horns, and heavy mane and glossy coat; and I felt the most exulting pride as I handled and examined him; for I had procured a trophy such as can fall henceforth to few hunters indeed.

— Excerpt abridged from Theodore Roosevelt, "The Bison or American Buffalo," *Hunting the Grisly and Other Sketches* (New York: The Review of Reviews Company, 1915), 3–36.

Shooting an Elk
on Two Ocean Pass

(1891)—Theodore Roosevelt

The future president stalks a magnificent bull by smell south of the park.

Although Theodore Roosevelt was an avid hunter, he favored prohibition of hunting inside Yellowstone National Park. The idea was that keeping hunters out would make the park an endless well of trophy animals that could be hunted outside its boundaries.

And Roosevelt knew that areas near the park provided marvelous hunting. One of them was the Two Ocean Pass, so named because a stream splits there, sending half its water to the Pacific and the other half to the Atlantic. Here's Roosevelt's description of one of his kills while hunting there in 1891.

The weather became clear and very cold, so that the snow made the frosty mountains gleam like silver. The moon was full, and in the flood of light the wild scenery round our camp was very beautiful. As always where we camped for several days, we had fixed long tables and settles, and were most comfortable; and when we came in at nightfall, or sometimes long afterward, cold, tired, and hungry, it was sheer physical delight to get warm before the roaring fire of pitchy stumps, and then to feast ravenously on bread and beans, on stewed or roasted elk venison, on grouse and sometimes trout, and flapjacks with maple syrup.

Next morning dawned clear and cold, the sky a glorious blue. Woody and I started to hunt over the great tableland, and led our stout horses up the mountainside, by elk trails so bad that they had to climb like goats. All these elk-trails have one striking peculiarity. They lead through thick timber, but every now and then send off short, well-worn branches to some cliff-edge or jutting crag, commanding a view far and wide over the country beneath. Elk love to stand on these lookout points, and scan the valleys and mountains round about.

Blue grouse rose from beside our path; Clarke's crows flew past us, with a hollow, flapping sound, or lit in the pine-tops, calling and flirting their tails; the gray-clad whiskeyjacks, with multitudinous cries, hopped and fluttered near us. Snowshoe rabbits scuttled away, the big furry feet, which give them their name already turning white. At last we came out on the great plateau, seamed with deep, narrow ravines. Reaches of pasture alternated with groves and open forests of varying size.

Almost immediately we heard the bugle of a bull elk, and saw a big band of cows and calves on the other side of a valley. There were three bulls with them, one very large, and we tried to creep up on them; but the wind was baffling and spoiled our stalk. So we returned to our horses, mounted them, and rode a mile farther, toward a large open wood on a hillside. When within 200 yards we heard directly ahead the bugle of a bull, and pulled up short.

In a moment I saw him walking through an open glade; he had not seen us. The slight breeze brought us down his scent. Elk have a strong characteristic smell; it is usually sweet, like that of a herd of Alderney cows; but in old bulls, while rutting, it is rank, pungent, and lasting. We stood motionless till the bull was out of sight, then stole to the wood, tied our horses, and trotted after him. He was traveling fast, occasionally calling, whereupon others in the neighborhood would answer. Evidently he had been driven out of some herd by the master bull.

He went faster than we did, and while we were vainly trying to overtake him we heard another very loud and sonorous challenge to our left. It came from a ridge-crest at the edge of the woods, among some scattered clumps of the northern nut-pine or pinyon—a queer conifer, growing very high on the mountains, its multi-forked trunk and wide-spreading branches giving it the rounded top, and, at a distance, the general look of an oak rather than a pine.

We at once walked toward the ridge, up-wind. In a minute or two, to our chagrin, we stumbled on an outlying spike bull, evidently kept on the outskirts of the herd by the master bull. I thought he would alarm all the rest; but, as we stood motionless, he could not see clearly what we were. He stood, ran, stood again, gazed at us, and trotted slowly off.

We hurried forward as fast as we dared, and with too little care, for we suddenly came in view of two cows. As they raised their heads to look, Woody squatted down where he was, to keep their attention fixed, while I cautiously tried to slip off to one side unobserved. Favored by the neutral tint of my buckskin hunting-shirt, with which my shoes, leggings, and soft hat matched, I succeeded. As soon as I was out of sight I ran hard and came up to a hillock crested with pinyons, behind which I judged I should find the herd.

As I approached the crest, their strong, sweet smell smote my nostrils. In another moment I saw the tips of a pair of mighty antlers, and I peered over the crest with my rifle at the ready. Thirty yards off, behind a clump of pinyons, stood a huge bull, his head thrown back as he rubbed his shoulders with his horns. There were several cows around him, and one saw me immediately, and took alarm. I fired into the bull's shoulder, inflicting a mortal wound; but he went off, and I raced after him at top speed, firing twice into his flank; then he stopped, very sick, and I broke his neck with a fourth bullet.

The elk I thus slew was a giant. His body was the size of a steer's, and his antlers, though not unusually long, were very massive and heavy. He lay in a glade, on the edge of a great cliff. Standing on its brink we overlooked a most beautiful country, the home of all homes for the elk: a wilderness of mountains, the immense evergreen forest broken by park and glade, by meadow and pasture, by bare hillside and barren tableland.

— Excerpt from Theodore Roosevelt, "An Elk Hunt at Two Ocean Pass," *The Wilderness Hunter: An Account of Big Game in the United States* (G. P. Putnam's Sons: New York, 1902), 177–202.

Buffalo Poacher Provokes a Law That Snares Him

(1894)—Captain George S. Anderson

*Rangers brave freezing weather
to apprehend a brazen buffalo poacher.*

*When the US Army took over administration of Yellowstone Park in 1886, one
of its primary missions was prevention of the poaching that was decimating the
wildlife. The soldiers worked hard to stop illegal hunting, but they lacked authority to do anything other than apprehend poachers, escort them out of the park, and
order them never to come back. Persistent poachers ignored the orders.*

*Finally, in 1894, a poacher was so brazen that he generated public attention
and forced Congress to act. Here's the park superintendent's account of how Ed
Howell's poaching career ended.*

Sometime in February I sent a scouting party across the Yellowstone and into
the Pelican Valley to look after the herds of buffalo and elk that usually winter there. On the return of this party they reported to me that they had found
an old snowshoe and toboggan trail, but that they were unable to follow it. It
apparently headed in the direction of Cooke City.

While this party was still out, word came to me that Ed Howell, a notorious poacher of Cooke City, had passed the Soda Butte Station one stormy
night and had gone on into Cooke for supplies, but that he had not carried
any of his trophies with him. A few days after this the sergeant in charge of
the Soda Butte Station reported the finding of a trail of this same party with
his toboggan and followed it as far as the park line.

I then determined on a plan that resulted in the capture of Howell. I
waited until I thought it was about time for him to be back in the Pelican

In the winter of 1894, soldiers captured a notorious poacher who was decimating the bison herd and confiscated trophies he was planning to sell. NATIONAL PARK SERVICE

country, and then sent out a large search party, with Captain Scott in charge. This party arrived at the Lake Hotel on the evening of March 11. Next day Burgess and Sergeant Troike of the Sixth Cavalry went over into the country previously indicated by me, and made their camp.

170

On the morning of the 13th, very soon after starting, they came across some old snowshoe tracks which they could scarcely follow, but by continuing in the direction of them they soon came across a cache of six bison scalps suspended above the ground, in the limbs of a tree.

Securing these trophies, the party continued on down Astringent Creek to its mouth and then turned down the Pelican. They soon came across a newly erected lodge, with evidences of occupation, and numerous snowshoe tracks in the vicinity.

Soon after this they were attracted by the sight of a man pursuing a herd of bison in the valley below them, followed by several shots from a rifle. After completing the killing, the culprit was seen to proceed with the removal of the scalps.

While thus occupied with the first one my scouting party ran upon him and made the capture. It turned out, as I had anticipated, to be Howell, who coolly remarked that if he had seen the party sooner they could never have captured him, meaning, of course, that he could have shot them before they were near enough to make effective the small pistol, which was the only weapon they carried. They brought him into this place as a prisoner, reaching here on the evening of the 16th of March.

I at once made full report of the affair and it was widely noted in the newspapers of the country. A suitable recognition, in the way of a certificate, was made of the coolness and bravery of Burgess and Troike. The scalps, as far as they could be saved, were brought in and properly prepared by a competent taxidermist and placed at the disposal of the department.

The feeling aroused in the minds of the public by this act of vandalism stirred Congress to prompt action, so that on May 7 an act for the protection of game in the park received the president's signature. In order that it may receive wider distribution, I enclose a copy to be printed with this report.

Howell denied having killed any bison but those found near him, but I feel sure that he did kill the six found in the cache, and it is quite probable that he killed others that we did not find. In one sense, it was the most fortunate thing that ever happened to the park, for it was surely the means of securing a law so much needed and so long striven for.

On April 25, Howell was released from confinement in the guardhouse by your order and removed from the park, and directed never again to return without proper permission. On the evening of July 28, I found him coolly sitting in the barber's chair in the hotel at this point. I instantly arrested him and reconfined him in the guardhouse, had him reported to the US attorney for this district, and on the evening of August 8, he received the first conviction under the law which he was instrumental in having passed. He was convicted before the commissioner of returning after expulsion, in violation of park regulations, and sentenced to confinement for one month and to a fine of $850.

With this conviction as a precedent and a strong determination to make other arrests under the new law whenever it is violated, I believe the days of poaching in the park are nearly at an end.

— Captain George S. Anderson, "Report of the Superintendent of Yellowstone National Park," *Executive Documents of the House of Representatives for the Third Session of the Fifty-Third Congress 1894–95* (Washington, DC: Government Printing Office, 1895), 657–658.

Hunting a Mountain Lion—
Anonymous

*"The men failed to see two pale green eyes
watching their every move."*

The secretary of the interior promulgated a regulation in 1883 that prohibited hunting in Yellowstone Park, but that was generally interpreted as not applying to predators. In fact the general policy toward predators—coyotes, wolves, bears, wolverines, and mountain lions—was "shoot on sight." Predators weren't protected in the park until the 1930s.

The story below was included as an example of student writing in a 1914 composition textbook for college freshmen. The textbook authors didn't give the student's name or the year the piece was written, but apparently it was after the army took over administration of Yellowstone in 1886.

"Whoa there! Back into the road, you black brute! What are you shyin' at?" yelled the driver of a sightseeing coach in the Yellowstone.

He glanced across the bridge and immediately learned the reason for the strange behavior of one of his leaders. There, in a leatherwood thicket, crouched the long, lithe form of a mountain lion. Its wicked yellow eyes challenged his right to the passage, and its long slender tail writhed among the bushes. The driver pulled up his horses, uncertain of the lion's intentions; but the great cat, finding himself unmolested, slipped through the bushes and disappeared among the jagged rocks on the mountain slope.

As the coach was discharging its passengers at the next stopping place, the driver yelled to a camp boy, "Go over and tell the guards I saw that big lion they've been looking for, down by the last bridge. Tell 'em they'd better hurry before he leaves the country."

The boy lost no time; and soon two of the soldiers were at the bridge, carefully examining the tracks of the great beast from the impressions in the loose dirt. They quickly learned that this lion was the very one with which they had been having a great deal of trouble, the one which had invaded camps during the night, and had terrified tourists with his long-drawn, almost human wail from the forests.

Clambering over the great grey rocks, and sliding in the loose gravel of the slope, the two soldiers made their way slowly up the mountainside. When they reached the first promontory they stopped to rest and look about them. Far to the left and a mile below them, still shrouded by the evening mists yet tinted now by the morning sun, lay the magnificent and awe-inspiring Yellowstone gorge. They gazed at the green thread winding along the floor of the great chasm and tried to hear what they knew to be the roar of its rushing waters.

"It's a great sight, Judd! We don't realize it, bein' here all the time. But come on. Let's hit the trail again."

"Wait a second," replied the other. "Help me tighten this bandage on my hand. It's come loose."

The men, intent upon the loosened bandage, failed to see that, from the edge of an overhanging rock above them, two pale green eyes were watching their every move. Behind the eyes, the sinewy form of a great cat was stealthily adjusting itself for a leap.

Having tightened the bandage, the men straightened up and at the same time stepped back a pace. Their feet, imbedded in the loose gravel, began to slide, and together the two soldiers rolled back under the overhanging rock. At the same instant a great tawny streak flashed over their heads, and the huge form of the mountain lion crashed into the rocks at the very place upon which they had been standing.

They jumped to their feet and, with startled eyes, watched the great ball of yellow fur as it bumped and rolled down the steep incline. The lion tore madly at the rocks and bushes as he fell, but tried in vain to secure a footing in the sliding gravel. A hundred feet below, he stopped with a thud against a fallen tree trunk; but before he could move, two bullets crunched their way through his body, and, with a gasp, he straightened out, dead.

— Anonymous, "A Yellowstone Lion," in Frances Berkeley Young and Karl Young, *Freshman English: A Manual* (New York: Henry Holt and Company, 1914), 561–562.

PART 10:
FISHING

INTRODUCTION

Fishing for sustenance and sport has always been an important part of the Yellowstone Experience.

Explorers traveling through Yellowstone Park in the 1870s pounced on every grasshopper they saw so they would have bait to catch fish for their evening supper. While their cook started a campfire and got bread baking, the travelers could catch their evening meal.

Early travelers found it easy to supplement their larders with fish from the lakes and streams in the Yellowstone watershed. But when they crossed the mountains to the Firehole River, they found the waters barren. Early travelers thought heat and chemicals from hot springs killed fish along the Firehole, but by the 1890s scientists concluded that was wrong. The new explanation was that physical barriers kept fish out. As rivers flowed off the hard lava rock that formed the Yellowstone Plateau, they carved waterfalls that fish couldn't climb.

The geologists' theory explained the fishless waters, but how did fish get into the upper Yellowstone? The answer, fish biologists decided, was that they came across the Two Ocean Pass south of the park where creeks cross the Continental Divide.

In 1889, officials began planting fish in the park, including exotic species such as rainbow, brook, lake, and brown trout. By 1955 more than 310 million native and nonnative fish had been planted in Yellowstone waters. The effort turned the once-barren waters into an anglers' paradise, but it also caused problems. Despite efforts to plan the process, inappropriate fish were introduced in many locations. Officials are still trying to straighten out the mess.

Early travelers reported great fishing around the Yellowstone River, and later travelers praised the results of planting fish around the Firehole River. Here are some of their stories.

A General Fights
to Land His First Fish

(1875)—General W. E. Strong

"The rod bent nearly double."

One of the most luxurious early trips to Yellowstone Park was led by President U. S. Grant's secretary of war, General William Belknap. In 1875 four other generals joined Belknap, including W. E. Strong, who provided an account of the trip.

The generals crossed the country in a plush Pullman car, smoking cigars, drinking whiskey, and telling stories, on the new transcontinental railroad. Then they rode in a special stagecoach that traveled at breakneck speed from Utah to Montana.

Along the way they were feted with banquets, parties, and parades. In Bozeman the Silver Coronet Band greeted them at the edge of town and escorted them through the city to Fort Ellis.

At Fort Ellis they were provided with an escort of active-duty soldiers led by Gustavus Doane, who had commanded the escort of the Washburn Expedition in 1870. Each general was assigned an orderly to take care of his every whim: packing his personal belongings, putting up his tent, rolling out his bed roll, digging his latrine, and cleaning any fish he caught—all at army expense, of course. A year later the US Senate impeached General Belknap for taking bribes.

General Strong eloquently describes the wonders of Yellowstone—falls, hot springs, and geysers—and the people he met: mountain men, stagecoach drivers, and townspeople. Most of all, he revels in telling exciting tales of hunting elk, stampeding buffalo, and catching fish. Here's his description of fishing.

Again I threw my hook in the swift water, and down the stream it went like lightning, tossing about like a feather in the rapid. My reel whirled and spun like a buzz saw, the line went out so fast.

I never touched the reel to check the running line till seventy-five feet, at least, was in the water. Then I pressed my thumb firmly upon it and drew gently back the rod. At the same instant something struck my hook that nearly carried me off my feet. I had to let go the reel to save the rod.

I had him securely hooked, but could I land him? That was the question. I gave him twenty-five or thirty feet more line—then checked again and tried to hold him—but it was no use, the rod bent nearly double, and I had to let him run.

My line was 150 feet in length, and I knew when it was all out, if the fish kept in the rapids, I should lose him. No tackle like mine could stand for a moment against the strength of such a fish as I had struck in such swift water.

I therefore continued to give him the line—but no faster than I was forced to. No more than twelve or fifteen feet remained on the reel. Fortunately for me, he turned to the left and was carried into an eddy that swept him into more quiet water near the shore.

Twice in his straight run down the rapid current of the stream he leaped clear from the water. I saw he was immense—something double or triple the size of any trout I had ever caught. The excitement to me was greater than anything I had ever experienced.

No one but a trout fisherman can understand or appreciate the intense pleasure of a single run. I was crazy to kill and land him, and yet I knew the chances were against it. Again and again I reeled him within twenty-five or thirty feet of the rock. But he was game to the last, and would dart off with the same strength as when he first struck. I had to let him go.

Finally, he showed signs of exhaustion. I managed to get him to top the water, and then worked him in close to the shore. Flynn was waiting to take the line and throw him out, as I had no landing net. Flynn did it very well. When the trout was very near the bank and quiet, he lifted him out.

He was a fine specimen, and would weigh four pounds if he weighed an ounce. This trout was three times the size I had ever caught. At 4:30 o'clock I stopped fishing having landed thirty-five trout which would have run from two and a half to four pounds in weight—none less than two and one half pounds.

— Excerpt abridged from W. E. Strong, *A Trip to the Yellowstone National Park in July, August, and September, 1875, From the Journal of W. E. Strong* (Washington, 1876), 61–62.

Fishing with Yankee Jim

(1889)—Rudyard Kipling

A famous English author swaps lies with the famous toll road operator and admires the fishing in Yankee Jim Canyon.

In 1889, when British author Rudyard Kipling visited Yellowstone, a spur of the Northern Pacific carried passengers from Livingston, Montana, to the edge of the park. But Kipling heeded advice from a fellow passenger and stopped to visit Yankee Jim George, the legendary operator of a toll road that ran through the canyon that still bears his name.

Yankee Jim was a garrulous man who must have met thousands of tourists after he began collecting tolls in 1873. Even after the county took over the road in 1887, travelers continued to stop by Yankee Jim's.

Dozens of travelers' diaries describe a stop at his cabin, note his courtly treatment of ladies, and recount his tall tales. Kipling was no exception. Here's his story.

From Livingston the National Park train follows the Yellowstone River through the gate of the mountains and over arid volcanic country. A stranger in the cars saw me look at the ideal trout-stream below the windows and murmured softly: "Lie off at Yankee Jim's if you want good fishing."

They halted the train at the head of a narrow valley, and I leaped literally into the arms of Yankee Jim, sole owner of a log hut, an indefinite amount of hay-ground, and constructor of twenty-seven miles of wagon-road over which he held toll right. There was the hut—the river fifty yards away, and the polished line of metals that disappeared round a bluff. That was all. The railway added the finishing touch to the already complete loneliness of the place.

Yankee Jim George operated a toll road in the canyon that still bears his name, and took in guests—including Rudyard Kipling—at his cabin there. GALLATIN HISTORY MUSEUM

Yankee Jim was a picturesque old man with a talent for yarns that Ananias might have envied. It seemed to me, presumptuous in my ignorance, that I might hold my own with the old-timer if I judiciously painted up a few lies gathered in the course of my wanderings. Yankee Jim saw every one of my tales and went fifty better on the spot.

He dealt in bears and Indians—never less than twenty of each; had known the Yellowstone country for years, and bore upon his body marks of Indian arrows; and his eyes had seen a squaw of the Crow Indians burned alive at the stake. He said she screamed considerable.

In one point did he speak the truth—as regarded the merits of that particular reach of the Yellowstone. He said it was alive with trout. It was. I fished it from noon till twilight, and the fish bit at the brown hook as though never a fat trout-fly had fallen on the water. From pebbly beaches, quivering in the heat-haze where the foot caught on stumps cut foursquare by the chisel-tooth of the beaver; past the fringe of the water-willow crowded with the breeding trout-fly and alive with toads and water-snakes; over the drifted timber to the grateful shadow of big trees that darkened the holes where the fattest fish lay, I worked for seven hours.

The mountain flanks on either side of the valley gave back the heat as the desert gives it, and the dry sand by the railway track, where I found a rattlesnake, was hot iron to the touch. But the trout did not care for the heat. They breasted the boiling river for my fly and they got it. I simply dare not give my bag. At the fortieth trout I gave up counting, and I had reached the fortieth in less than two hours. They were small fish—not one over two pounds—but they fought like small tigers, and I lost three flies before I could understand their methods of escape. Ye gods! That was fishing.

— Excerpt from Rudyard Kipling, *From Sea to Sea: Letters of Travel,* Volume Two (New York: Doubleday & McClure Company, 1899), 203-205.

The Mystery of the Fishless Waters

(1896)—Barton Warren Evermann

A biologist describes the spot where fish cross from the Pacific to Atlantic watersheds.

Early travelers to the area that became Yellowstone National Park found fish were abundant in the Yellowstone River and Lake and their tributaries, but many other lakes and streams were devoid of fish. At first people thought heat and chemicals from geothermal features killed fish in some places. Then geologists offered another explanation.

The Yellowstone Plateau, geologists said, was a huge sheet of volcanic rock left by a super volcano. Across eons, a giant glacier formed over the volcanic rock. When the ice age ended, the glacier melted, washing away soft material but leaving hard volcanic rock. This formed a circle of waterfalls and cascades that fish couldn't get over to populate the plateau.

The geologists' theory explained the fishless waters, but it left a deeper mystery: How did fish get into upper Yellowstone and its tributaries? Certainly they didn't do it by climbing the three-hundred-foot Lower Falls of the Yellowstone.

Then people remembered mountain man Jim Bridger's tale of the "Two Ocean Pass," a place on the headwaters of the Yellowstone where creeks crossed the Continental Divide. Explorers had documented the existence of the pass, but it wasn't until 1891 that the US Fish Commission sent an ichthyologist to the area.

Here's how Dr. Barton Warren Evermann described what he found at Two Ocean Pass.

We stood upon the bank of either fork of Atlantic Creek, just above the place of the "parting of the waters," and watched the stream pursue its rapid but dangerous and uncertain course along the very crest of the "Great Continental

Divide." A creek flowing along the ridgepole of a continent is unusual and strange, and well worth watching and experimenting with.

We waded to the middle of the North Fork, and, lying down upon the rocks in its bed, we drank the pure icy water that was hurrying to the Pacific. Without rising, but by simply bending a little to the left, we took a draught from that portion of the stream that was just deciding to go east, via the Missouri-Mississippi route, to the Gulf of Mexico.

And then we tossed chips, two at a time, into the stream. Though they would strike the water within an inch or so of each other, not infrequently one would be carried by the current to the left, keeping in Atlantic Creek, while the other might be carried a little to the right and enter the branch running across the meadow to Pacific Creek; the one beginning a journey which will finally bring it to the Great Gulf, the other entering upon a long voyage in the opposite direction to Balboa's ocean.

Pacific Creek is a stream of good size long before it enters the pass, and its course through the meadow is in a definite channel; but not so with Atlantic Creek. The west bank of each fork is low, and the water is liable to break through anywhere, and thus send a part of its water across to Pacific Creek. It is probably true that one or two branches always connect the two creeks under ordinary conditions, and that, following heavy rains, or when the snows are melting, a much greater portion of the water of Atlantic Creek finds its way across the meadow to the other.

It is certain that there is, under ordinary circumstances, a continuous waterway through Two Ocean Pass of such a character as to permit fishes to pass easily and readily from Snake River over to the Yellowstone, or in the opposite direction. Indeed, it is possible, barring certain falls in Snake River, for a fish so inclined to start at the mouth of the Columbia, travel up that great river to its principal tributary, the Snake, thence on through the long, tortuous course of that stream, and, under the shadows of the Grand Tetons, enter the cold waters of Pacific Creek, by which it could journey on up to the very crest of the Great Continental Divide to Two Ocean Pass; through this pass it may have a choice of two routes to Atlantic Creek, in which the down-stream journey is begun. Soon it reaches the Yellowstone, down which it continues to Yellowstone Lake, then through the lower Yellowstone out into the turbid waters of the Missouri. For many hundred miles, it may continue down this mighty river before reaching the Father of Waters, which will finally carry it to the Gulf of Mexico—a wonderful journey of nearly six thousand miles, by far the longest possible fresh-water journey in the world.

We found trout in Pacific Creek at every point where we examined it. In Two Ocean Pass, we obtained specimens from each of the streams, and in such positions as would have permitted them to pass easily from one side of the divide to the other. We also caught trout in Atlantic Creek below the pass, and in the upper Yellowstone, where they were abundant.

Thus it is certain that there is no obstruction even in dry weather to prevent the passage of trout from the Snake River to Yellowstone Lake; it is quite evident that trout do pass over in this way; and it is almost absolutely certain that Yellowstone Lake was stocked with trout from the west, via Two Ocean Pass.

— Excerpt adapted from Barton Warren Evermann, "Two Ocean Pass," *Inland Educator* 2, no. 6 (July 1896): 299–306.

A Woman Trout Fishing in Yellowstone Park

(1897)—Mary T. Townsend

A woman catches fish of several species that were planted in the Firehole River.

Early explorers discovered many stretches of water in Yellowstone Park were devoid of fish. Efforts to stock the barren waters with exotic fish caused ecological problems that officials are still trying to fix, but they also resulted in an anglers' paradise.

Soon people from all over the world were coming to Yellowstone Park to fish and reporting phenomenal catches. Here's one woman's story about fishing a once-barren stretch of the Firehole River.

In 1888, the United States Fish Commission stocked the Firehole with many varieties of trout. They are still uneducated, eager for the fly; a number six or eight gray professor or brown Montreal proved the most killing. The father of all the Pacific trout, the black-spotted or "cut-throat" (*Salmo mykiss*), with the scarlet splotch on his lower jaw, was most in evidence. With long, symmetrical body and graduated black spots on his burnished sides, he is a brave, dashing fighter, often leaping salmon-like many times from the water before he can be brought to creel. We found him feeding in the open riffs, or rising on the clear surface of some sunlit pool. "The pleasantest angling is to see the fish cut with her golden oars the silver stream."

Our dainty eastern trout, with brilliant red spots and short, thick-set body, had hardly become accustomed to the change from grass-edged streams and sheltered pools, to the fierce struggle for existence in this fire-bound river. The glint of his white-edged fins betrayed him swaying in the eddies at the foot of some big rock or hidden in the shade of an overhanging bank, thereby offering a direct contrast to his more aggressive western cousin.

The California rainbow trout proved true to his reputation, as absolutely eccentric and uncertain, sometimes greedily taking a fly, and again refusing to be tempted by the most brilliant array of a carefully stocked book. During several days' fishing we landed some small ones, none weighing over two pounds, although they are said to have outstripped the other varieties in rapidity of growth, and tales were told of four-pounders landed by more favored anglers.

A heavy splash, a ray of silvery light, and with lengthened line the fly was carefully dropped on the surface of a swirling pool, edged with water-plants and tangled grasses, where the current had gullied out deep holes around the big boulders; a rise, a strike—now for a fight.

Long dashes down stream taxed my unsteady footing; the sharp click and whirr of the reel resounded in desperate efforts to hold him somewhat in check; another headlong dash, then a vicious bulldog shake of the head as he sawed back and forth across the rocks. Every wile inherited from generations of wily ancestors was tried until, in a moment of exhaustion, the net was slipped under him. Wading ashore with my prize, I had barely time to notice his size—a good four-pounder, and unusual markings, large yellow spots encircled by black, with great brilliancy of iridescent color—when back he flopped into the water and was gone. However, I took afterward several of the same variety, known in the park as the Von Baer trout, and which I have since found to be the *Salmo fario*, the veritable trout of Izaak Walton.

So, on down the stream, careful placing of the fly and changing of the feathers brought different varieties to the surface. One other fish proved a complete surprise. He was of silvery gray color, covered with small black crescents. Some of the park fishermen called him a Norwegian trout; others, the Loch Leven. Any country might be proud to claim him, with his harmonious proportions, game fighting qualities and endurance.

As the river had worn a pathway around the formation much too deep for wading, I climbed around the edge, past its heated springs and over its mosaic paving, and was seldom disappointed in coaxing a rise where the hot sulphur-tainted streams dripped into the water of the Firehole.

When my creel became uncomfortably heavy, and square spotted tails began to overlap its edge, I waded ashore to look at my catch. Fortunately my

Some lucky hotel employees in Yellowstone Park had the job of supplying the kitchen with enough fish to provide dinner for all the guests. NATIONAL PARK SERVICE

boots were heavy, for the bank was honeycombed with miniature geysers and mud-pots, bubbling and sputtering in wicked imitation of their bigger sisters. My last captive being still on my line, I swung it from the river into a geyser cone. Unprepared for the temperature, my return cast brought out only a hook with skull and backbone attached; the flesh had instantly boiled off.

Surfeited with success, I unjointed my much tried and highly prized Mitchell rod, a veritable Japanese jiujutsu, "to conquer by yielding," among fly rods. It can never more be duplicated, now that the master who engrafted his love of stream, of woods, of trout, into the rod he fashioned, has passed from sight around the bend of life's stream, beyond which we cannot follow him.

— Excerpt from Mary T. Townsend, "A Woman's Trout Fishing in Yellowstone Park." *Outing: An Illustrated Magazine of Sport, Travel and Recreation* 30 (1897): 165–177.

Fishing the Once-Barren Firehole River

(1897)—Frank B. King

"Something struck the end fly and started upstream, making the line hum through the water and the reel spin."

Early travelers assumed the reason that some lakes and streams in Yellowstone Park were barren of fish was because of hot water and chemicals from springs and geysers. However, in 1889, officials initiated a program of stocking fish, which proved that physical barriers like waterfalls caused the problem.

By the late 1890s, when Frank B. King and his friend hauled their fly rods and creels through the park, the once-barren rivers and lakes were teeming with fish. King had been traveling through the park for several days before he arrived at the Firehole River and finally got an opportunity to test the famous fishing waters of Yellowstone Park. Here's his story of what happened then.

When we reached the park, every one told us we could catch fish anywhere and everywhere, but still those rods remained under the seat, and as the days passed by, we wished we could tell some of those people what we thought of them. When we looked into the hot springs, we saw no signs of fish, and in the geysers the finny tribe was missing.

Still we went bravely on, now and then casting a longing glance at the rods, and hoping, at least, that we might some day find some place where we could take them out of their cases and look at them, if nothing more.

As we turned our backs upon Old Faithful and his companions that afternoon, and drove down the Firehole River toward the Fountain house, the shadows were just commencing to lengthen. Through the pines, I could catch here and there tantalizing glimpses of the river as it ran along between its meadowy banks. Now and then, it formed rapids that ran into beautiful pools and then out again into long, open riffles. Here, there would be a log extending out into the water, at the end of which I could see a tempting eddy from which I was almost sure I could coax a "big one." Next, there would be a long bend with a riffle above and below it. In those riffles, I could imagine I saw several "beauties" waiting for a fly to drop upon the water that they might jump at it.

Well, I stood all this just as long as I could. I was going to get out my rod and make a try, even if I failed. My companion was a little, in fact, very sleepy, and did not care whether there were fish or no fish; what he had his mind on was that long, quiet nap he was to have when he reached the hotel. By promising him that I would only make a few casts, and that he could sleep in the surrey while I tried my luck, he consented to wait just a minute or two.

I pulled on some overalls, a fishing-coat, a pair of "gums"; set up my pet rod; tried the reel to see if it still knew its song; ran the line through the guides; tied on a leader; picked a brown hackle, a royal coachman, and a black gnat, out of my book; and sallied down to the river. Before me was a beautiful pool, one of those long, deep ones with just enough current running through it to make the flies work well.

I crept up as close to the pool as I dared, took the rod in my right hand, and made a long, pretty cast out past the middle of the pool. The flies had no sooner straightened out than there was a break in the water and a streak of gold and black passed over the end hackle and into the water. He had missed it; but he was a beauty. I felt like letting out an Indian whoop—there was a fish in the river anyway, I had seen him. The next thing to do was to catch him.

I was all of a tremble, for if ever I wanted a fish in my life, I wanted that one, if for nothing more than to give me some cause for yelling to my sleepy companion to bring down the landing net. Once more I drew back and made a long cast, but the flies struck a little too far upstream and had to travel with the current a little distance.

No sooner were they over the spot where I had had the first rise than, zip, something struck the end fly and started upstream, making the line hum through the water and the reel spin. I did not think, as some people tell, that I had a whale or an elephant, I knew what it was—it was a good big trout. There is only one thing that acts the way this something on the end of my line did, and that is a gamey trout.

He ran upstream until the current and strain of the rod was too much, and then he left the water. You can imagine the way he left the water. You know the way a big trout acts. Well, he acted as they all do. When he was back in the water, he started down stream, and when he reached the end of the pool, he broke again and then came toward me and then away from me.

By this time, the first rush was over and I let out a long, deep yell for my sleepy friend. As soon as he heard that yell, he knew just what was up, and he came down that hill with the landing net in his hand just as fast as a man who was not a bit sleepy. His first words were:

"What have you got? How big is he?"

After a little sulking, a few dashes, and a break or two, came the fight around the landing net, and at last I had him kicking in the grass on the bank. He was a beauty! A Loch Leven that measured nearly twenty inches and weighed over two pounds and a half. As he lay there in the grass, his yellow stripe and red spots upon the black made a very pretty picture. He was a beauty, and he was ours.

Thoughts of a nap left the mind of my companion, and fishing was declared the order of the day. He soon had his "Leonard" set up, and before many minutes had a mate to mine bending it almost double. I never saw any one wake up so quickly in my life. He never had a thought of sleep the rest of the afternoon. The fact was he did not have time for such thoughts, the fish kept him too busy.

From the time I hooked my first fish up to a little while before dark, we had the finest fishing I ever heard of. When I say it was the finest fishing I ever heard of, I mean it, and I have heard some very tall fish stories. We fished side by side all afternoon and one was working with fish all the time, and part of the time both of us had our hands full.

We lost the biggest one we had hooked, of course; one always does. When we left the stream, we had twenty-two fish that would average over two pounds apiece. Some were rainbows; some were Loch Levens; some were cutthroats, and they were all beauties, every one of them a work of art. I never hope to catch such a gamey, beautiful mess of trout again. Such fishing one only has once in a lifetime.

— Excerpt from Frank B. King, "In Nature's Laboratory: Driving and Fishing in Yellowstone Park," *Overland Monthly*, 29, no. 174 (June 1897): 594–603.

PART 11:
BEAR STORIES

INTRODUCTION

Hunting, watching, and photographing bears.

Bears are resilient creatures that adapt quickly to their surroundings. Early travelers found these top predators fearless, which made hunting them great sport. But bears soon discovered that men with guns are dangerous, so sightings became rare by the 1880s.

In 1886 the army took over administration of the park and began enforcing a no-guns policy. Soon animals that had fled from public view to avoid slaughter reappeared where tourists could see them.

After the Yellowstone Park Company built luxury hotels, kitchen managers began dumping scraps in the nearby woods. Soon bears began feeding at these dumps, and tourists came to see the bears. By the 1890s, bear watching at dumps became one of Yellowstone's must-see activities and campers had to be careful to protect their food from the prowling beasts.

The Park Service admitted cars in 1915, and bears soon discovered they could approach travelers who didn't have horses to scare. Bear jams began to back up roads for miles as tourists stopped to feed the animals and watch their antics.

With bears and people in such close proximity, injuries were common, so the Park Service began developing policies to keep them apart. By the early 1970s, bear sightings became rare as the rangers closed dumps, enforced "do not feed the bears" regulations, and began hauling pesky animals to the backcountry. Today park visitors consider themselves lucky if they see a bear. But as these stories attest, that wasn't always true.

Colonel Pickett Gets His First Bear

(1877)—Jack Bean

A guide fires five Winchester balls into a bear to help a Confederate colonel make his first kill.

After word spread about the magnificent big game in Yellowstone Park, hunters from the eastern United States and Europe began coming to bag a trophy. Even if they were skilled hunters where they came from, they needed someone to guide them in the rugged West. Jack Bean had the perfect credentials for the job. Before hiring out as a guide, Bean had been a trapper, hunter, and Indian fighter.

In the summer of 1877, the army hired Bean to look for Chief Joseph and his band of Nez Perce Indians along the Madison River and in Yellowstone Park. When he returned to Bozeman after locating the Indians and telling the army they were headed into Yellowstone Park, he discovered a Colonel Pickett wanted to hire him as a hunting guide. In his memoir Bean tells this tale about the intrepid colonel.

Our trail led us over Mount Washburn where it commenced to snow. By the time we had reached our highest point in the trail the snow was about a foot deep. As the colonel had only summer shoes, he had to walk to keep warm. So the colonel stopped to dig the snow off his shoes and tie them a little tighter. I looked back behind me and saw a big bear crossing the trail. I spoke to the colonel, "There goes a bear." But he kept tying his shoe. When he had finished he raised his head and with a southern accent answered me, "Whar?"

I advised him that a bear didn't wait for a man to tie his shoe. Our trail now left the ridge and descended down to the head of Tower Creek where we saw another big bear in the trail coming toward us. So I told the colonel, "There comes a bear."

"Whar?" he answered so I showed him. He got off his horse and walked quietly up the trail. I watched Mr. Bear and saw him leave the trail and start up the grassy hillside.

Jack Bean was a trapper, scout, and Indian fighter before he began guiding hunters into Yellowstone Park. GALLATIN HISTORY MUSEUM

I was afraid that the colonel would shoot him when the bear was right above him and it would come down and use him rather roughly. The colonel saw him when he was on the hillside about 30 yards away, so I dismounted and slipped up behind the colonel. When the colonel shot the bear it made a big growl and came down the hill on the run and passed him within 30 feet. The colonel didn't know I was so close behind him until I spoke.

I told him to hold his fire until the bear jumped the creek, but he wouldn't do it. As the bear passed the colonel shot and missed him. When the bear crossed the creek I opened fire with my Winchester. By the time the colonel could load and was ready to shoot again I had put five Winchester balls into him. But the colonel gave him his last shot through the breast while the bear was falling. It rolled into the creek dead.

We found when we had examined the bear that the colonel's first shot just went under the skin in the bear's neck, which caused him to come down the hill so rapidly.

I knew that the colonel would want to take this hide along. But we only had one packhorse between the two of us and it was too loaded to carry the wet and green hide. So I decided that I had better spoil it. So I gave my knife a lick on the steel and as we got to the bear I stuck my knife between the ears and split the skin down the backbone clean to the tail.

The colonel gave me a slap on the back and says, "Bean, that's my bear."

I told him, "All right." It was no credit to me to kill a bear.

"Well," he says, "We'll take this skin."

I said, "Why didn't you say so before I split the skin—why I've spoiled it."

The colonel was very much put out to lose the skin. He tramped the snow down for ten feet around and finally concluded he would take the front paw and hind foot and a good chunk of meat to eat. I only took meat enough for him, as I didn't care for bear meat. And after dissecting the bear we journeyed on our way to the Yellowstone falls and made camp.

That night he wanted me to cook him plenty of bear meat, but I cooked bacon for myself. I noticed that after chewing the bear meat a little, he would throw it out of his mouth when he thought I wasn't looking. I gave him bear meat for about two days and throwed the balance away, which was never inquired for.

— Adapted from Jack Bean, "Real Hunting Tales," Typescript, Gallatin History Museum, 29–31.

The Colonel's Version of Bagging His First Bear

(1877)—Colonel William D. Pickett

A Confederate colonel tells his version of bagging his first bear.

When two people describe the same event, interesting differences often occur. That certainly happened when Colonel William D. Pickett and his guide, Jack Bean, described the colonel's first bear hunt.

The hunt happened shortly after the Nez Perce Indians fled through Yellowstone Park following the bloody Big Hole Battle on August 9, 1877. Although there was still a possibility of danger from Indians remaining in the park, Pickett was eager to hunt for grizzly bears there, so he hired Jack Bean, an old Indian fighter and frontiersman, as his guide.

Bean's version of their trip is presented in the preceding story. Here's how Colonel Pickett, who later became a famous bear hunter, described his first kill.

It was learned the hostile Indians had passed through the national park, followed by Howard's forces. As there was still time to make a hasty trip through the Park before the severe winter set in, I determined to do so. I was urged not to make the attempt on account of the hostiles' sick or wounded that might have been left behind, and of other Indians. I recognized the risk, but since as a youngster I had served during the Mexican War as a mounted volunteer on the northwest frontier of Texas against the Comanches, and all the bad Indians of the Indian Territory and of the Kansas Territory who infested that frontier, I had some knowledge of Indian ways. Added to this, was the experience of four years' service in the War Between the States. These experiences qualified me to judge of the credence to be placed in war rumors. I was anxious to make the trip.

Only one man of suitable qualities could be found willing to make the trip—Jack Bean. He knew the routes through the park; he was a good packer and mountain man, cautious, but resolute. We went light. I rode my hunting mare, Kate; Jack his horse, and we packed my little red mule, Dolly. I was armed with a .45-90-450 Sharpe long-range rifle, and Jack with a .44-40-200 repeater. In addition to a belt of cartridges, Bean carried around his neck a shot bag pretty full of cartridges, so that in case of being set afoot, they would be handy. When Dolly was packed there was not much visible except her ears and feet.

We left Bozeman September 11, and nooned in the second canyon of the Yellowstone on the 13th. While there, a portion of the cavalry that accompanied Colonel Gilbert on his trip around from the head of the Madison, passed down toward Fort Ellis, having with them Cowan and Albert Oldham, who had survived the hostile Indians near the Lower Geyser Basin.

In the afternoon, we passed up the river, by the cabin of Henderson, burned by hostiles, turned up Gardner River and camped within three miles of Mammoth Hot Springs. As this squad of cavalry passed down, we were conscious that we had to depend entirely on our own resources for the remainder of the trip, for there was probably not another white man in the park. A note in my diary says: "International rifle match commences today."

Early on the 14th, we went on to Mammoth Hot Springs, and spent two or three hours viewing their beauties and wonders. We passed by the cabin, in the door of which the Helena man had been killed a few days before, after having escaped the attack on the camp above the grand falls. During the day's travel, there were splendid mountain views from the trail.

In the afternoon of September 15, the trail descended to the valley of the Yellowstone and passed within one mile of Baronett's Bridge, across which Howard's command passed on the 5th of September in pursuit of the Nez Perces. We soon dropped into the trail taken by that command and followed it back to Tower Fall.

September 16, we packed up and began the ascent of the Mount Washburn range. For a few miles, the trail followed an open ridge, exposing us to a northeast blizzard, accompanied by snow. After descending into the gulch, up which the trail leads to the pass in the range, the snow became deeper, and toward the summit of the range, it was eighteen or twenty inches, knee-deep, which compelled us to dismount and lead the horses, as the ascent was very hard on them. In view of future possibilities, we made every effort to save their strength. It was one of the most laborious day's work of my experience.

When near the summit, going through open pine timber, we discovered a large bear approaching us. He was moving along the side of the steep mountain to the left, about on a level, and would have passed out of safe range. I immediately dismounted and cut across as rapidly as the snow and the ascent admitted, to intercept him. He had not discovered us. When within about one hundred yards, watching my opportunity through the timber, I fired at his side. He was hit, but not mortally. As my later experience told me, those bears when hit always either roll down hill or go "on the jump." On the jump this bear came, passing about twenty yards in our front. A cartridge was ready, and against Jack's injunction "Don't shoot," I fired; yet, it failed to stop him, and Jack turned loose with his repeater, I shooting rapidly with my rifle. By the time the bear had reached the gulch he stopped, to go no further.

The excitement caused by this incident and my enthusiasm on killing my first grizzly—for I claimed the bear—dispelled at once all feelings of hardship and fatigue. The bear was a grizzly of about 400 pounds weight, fat and with a fine pelt. We had not time to skin him, nor could the hide have been packed. After getting a few steaks, a piece of skin from over the shoulder and one of his forepaws, we continued our laborious ascent of the mountain. Still excited by this incident, the work was now in the nature of a labor of love.

— Abridged from William D. Pickett, *Hunting at High Altitudes*, George Bird Grinnell, ed. (Harper & Brothers: New York, 1913), 62–68.

Bears Fight at a Dump

(1898)—Ernest Thompson Seton

A momma bear takes on a grizzly to protect her sickly cub.

When luxury hotels began dumping garbage in nearby forests, bear watching became as popular with tourists as viewing geysers. One tourist who went to the park to watch bears was the famous wildlife artist, naturalist, and writer Ernest Thompson Seton.

Seton, who helped found the Boy Scouts of America, not only wrote the first Boy Scout Handbook, *he also wrote and illustrated popular stories about wild animals for magazines and books. Nearly every boy and girl in America knew about Seton and his stories.*

In 1897 he came to Yellowstone Park to do an inventory of large animals for a magazine that focused on wildlife conservation. On that trip Seton saw a fight between a grizzly and a momma black bear protecting her invalid cub that everybody called "Johnny." Seton's story about the fight became the basis for his most famous story, "Johnny Bear." Seton was so fond of the story that he told it a second time from the perspective of Wahb, the subject of his book Biography of a Grizzly.

"Johnny Bear" originally appeared in Scribner's *magazine and was republished in Seton's book,* Wild Animals I Have Known. *The following is a condensed version.*

All the jam pots were at Johnny's end; he stayed by them, and Grumpy stayed by him. At length he noticed that his mother had a better tin than any he could find, and, as he ran whining to take it from her, he chanced to glance away up the slope. There he saw something that made him sit up and utter a curious little *Koff Koff Koff Koff Koff.*

His mother turned quickly, and sat up to see "what the child was looking at" I followed their gaze, and there, oh horrors! was an enormous grizzly bear. He was a monster; he looked like a fur-clad omnibus coming through the trees.

Johnny set up a whine at once and got behind his mother. She uttered a deep growl, and all her back hair stood on end. Mine did too, but I kept as still as possible.

With stately tread the grizzly came on. His vast shoulders sliding along his sides, and his silvery robe swaying at each tread, like the trappings on an elephant, gave an impression of power that was appalling.

Johnny began to whine more loudly, and I fully sympathized with him now, though I did not join in. After a moment's hesitation Grumpy turned to her noisy cub and said something that sounded to me like two or three short coughs—*Koff Koff Koff.* But I imagine that she really said, "My child, I think you had better get up that tree, while I go and drive the brute away."

At any rate, that was what Johnny did.

Grumpy stalked out to meet the grizzly. She stood as high as she could and set all her bristles on end; then, growling and chopping her teeth, she faced him.

The grizzly, so far as I could see, took no notice of her. He came striding toward the feast as though alone. But when Grumpy got within twelve feet of him she uttered a succession of short, coughy roars, and, charging, gave him a tremendous blow on the ear. The grizzly was surprised; but he replied with a left-hander that knocked her over like a sack of hay.

Nothing daunted, but doubly furious, she jumped up and rushed at him. Then they clinched and rolled over and over, whacking and pounding, snorting and growling, and making no end of dust and rumpus. But above all their noise I could clearly hear Little Johnny, yelling at the top of his voice, and evidently encouraging his mother to go right in and finish the grizzly at once.

She scrambled over and tried to escape. But the grizzly was mad now. He meant to punish her, and dashed around the root. For a minute they kept up a dodging chase about it; but Grumpy was quicker of foot, and somehow always managed to keep the root between herself and her foe, while Johnny, safe in the tree, continued to take an intense and uproarious interest.

At length, seeing he could not catch her that way, the grizzly sat up on his haunches; and while he doubtless was planning a new move, old Grumpy saw her chance, and making a dash, got away from the root and up to the top of the tree where Johnny was perched.

— Excerpt from Ernest Thompson Seton, "Johnny Bear" *Scribner's* 28, no. 6 (December 1900): 658–671.

For Yellowstone Park's first hundred years, bears wandered freely through campgrounds, entertaining travelers and occasionally creating havoc. NATIONAL PARK SERVICE

Watching a Giant Grizzly

(1898)—Grace Gallatin Seton

A famous writer/naturalist's wife finds her husband hiding in a garbage dump to watch bears.

In 1915 a giant grizzly that roamed between the Meeteetsee region of Wyoming and Yellowstone Park was so well-known that the New York Times *published the news that he had been shot to death. He was Wahb, a bear made famous by the naturalist and writer Ernest Thompson Seton. Seton described Wahb in his popular book,* Biography of a Grizzly, *and in his story "Johnny Bear."*

Seton's wife, Grace Gallatin Seton, also wrote about Wahb. In her version Grace called her husband "Nimrod," after the mighty hunter of the Bible. She called A. A. Anderson, the owner of the ranch where she first saw Wahb's tracks, "the Host." Here's Grace's story.

A fourteen-inch track is big, even for a grizzly. That was the size of Wahb's. The first time I saw it, the hole looked big enough for a baby's bathtub. The Host said there was only one bear in that region that could make a track like that; in spite of the fact that this was beyond his range, it must be Meeteetsee Wahb. He got off his horse and measured the track. Yes, the hind foot tracked fourteen inches. What a hole in the ground it looked!

The Host said the maker of it was probably far away, as he judged the track to be several weeks old. I had heard so many tales of this monster that when I gazed upon his track I felt as though I were looking at the autograph of a hero.

It was not till the next year that I really saw Wahb. It was at his summer haunt, the Fountain Hotel in Yellowstone National Park. If you were to ask Nimrod to describe the Fountain Geyser or Hell Hole, or any of the other tourist sights thereabouts, I am sure he would shake his head and tell you there was nothing but bears around the hotel. For this was the occasion when Nimrod spent the entire day in the garbage heap watching the bears, while I did the conventional thing and saw the sights.

About sunset, I got back to the hotel. Much to my surprise, I could not find Nimrod; and neither had he been seen since morning, when he had started in the direction of the garbage heap in the woods some quarter of a mile back from the hotel. Anxiously I hurried there, but could see no Nimrod. Instead, I saw the outline of a grizzly feeding quietly on the hillside. It was very lonely and gruesome.

Under other circumstances, I certainly would have departed quickly the way I came, but now I must find Nimrod. It was growing dark, and the bear looked a shocking size, as big as a whale. Dear me, perhaps Nimrod was inside—Jonah style. Just then, I heard a sepulchral whisper from the earth.

"Keep quiet, don't move, it's the big grizzly."

I looked about for the owner of the whisper and discovered Nimrod not far away in a nest he had made for himself in a pile of rubbish. I edged nearer.

"See, over there in the woods are two black bears. You scared them away. Isn't he a monster?" indicating Wahb.

I responded with appropriate enthusiasm. Then after a respectful silence, I ventured to say:

"How long have you been here?"

"All day—and such a day—thirteen bears at one time. It is worth all your geysers rolled into one."

"H'm—Have you had anything to eat?"

"No." Another silence, then I began again.

"Aren't you hungry? Don't you want to come to dinner?"

He nodded yes. Then I sneaked away and came back as soon as possible with a change of clothes. The scene was as I had left it, but duskier. I stood waiting for the next move. The grizzly made it. He evidently had finished his meal for the night, and now moved majestically off up the hill towards the pinewoods. At the edge of these he stood for a moment, Wahb's last appearance, so far as I am concerned, for, as he posed, the fading light dropped its curtain of darkness between us, and I was able to get Nimrod away.

— Abridged from Grace Gallatin Seton, "What I Know About Wahb of the Big Horn Basin," *A Woman Tenderfoot* (Doubleday, Page and Co.: New York, 1900).

Photographing Grizzlies
with Flash Powder

(1906)—William Henry Wright

*William Henry Wright tests his new method
of nighttime photography on grizzlies.*

At the dawn of the twentieth century, a self-described hunter-naturalist named William Henry Wright decided to start carrying a camera on his various expeditions. He soon began taking excursions just to photograph animals. After a while, he decided to take on the challenges of photographing grizzlies.

Because the grizzlies are shy and tend to be nocturnal, Wright said, chances of taking a daylight photo were slim, so he began experimenting with ways to use batteries and tripwires to ignite flash powder. By 1906 he had perfected his techniques enough to go to Yellowstone Park to try them out. It took several attempts before Wright succeeded in getting a decent photograph. Here's his description of his first try.

I followed some of the more travelled trails for several miles and found that nearly all of the grizzlies had their headquarters in the range of mountains around Mount Washburn. I then selected their largest highway, and after setting up my camera, concealed myself one evening about a hundred feet from the trail and to leeward of it, and watched for the coming of the grizzlies. Across the trail I had stretched a number forty sewing thread, one end attached to the electric switch and the other to a small stake driven into the ground beyond the trail. Just below where I had located, there was an open park in which the bears had been feeding, as was shown by the grass that had been nipped and the holes that had been dug for roots.

For some hours I waited in the bushes and fought gnats and mosquitoes. I saw several black bears pass along the hillside, but not a grizzly showed his nose until after the sun had set and the little marsh in the park was covered with a mantle of fog. Suddenly then, far up the trail, appeared what at first looked like a shadow, so slowly and silently did it move. But I knew at once, by the motion of the head and the long stride, that a grizzly was coming to the bottom for a few roots and a feed of grass.

I was, of course, very anxious to see what he would do when he came to the thread across the trail, and I had not long to wait, for he came on steadily but slowly and, when within ten feet of the thread, he stopped, poked out his nose and sniffed two or three times, raised up on his hind feet, took a few more sniffs, and then bolted up the trail in the direction from which he had come.

A few minutes after he had gone, three more appeared. These were evidently of one litter and appeared to be between two and three years old. They came on with the same cautious movements, and when they were close upon the thread, they also stopped and went through a similar performance. The one in front pushed out his nose and sniffed gingerly at the suspicious object. Those in the rear also stopped, but being curious to learn what was causing the blockade, the second one placed his forefeet on the rump of the one in front, in order to see ahead, while the third one straightened up on his hind legs and looked over the other two.

They made a beautiful group, and just as they had poised themselves, the one in front must have touched the string a little harder than he had intended to, for there was a sudden flash that lit up the surroundings, and I expected to see the bears go tearing off through the timber, but, to my utter surprise, nothing of the kind happened.

They all three stood up on their hind legs, and looked at each other as much as to say, "Now, what do you think of that?" and then they took up their investigation where it had been interrupted, followed the thread to where it was fastened to the stick, clawed up the spool, which I had buried in the ground, sniffed at it, and then went back to the trail, where they had first found the thread. Here they again stood up, and then, having either satisfied their curiosity or becoming suspicious, they turned around and trailed away through the timber.

As far as I could see them they went cautiously, and stopped at frequent intervals to stand up and look behind them to see if there were any more flashes or if anything was following them. Unfortunately this picture was utterly worthless. I had failed to use enough flash powder, and when I came to develop the plate, it showed only the dimmest outline of the animals.

— Excerpt from William Henry Wright, *The Grizzly Bear: The Narrative of a Hunter Naturalist* (New York: Scribner's Sons, 1909), 144–146.

TR Described Yellowstone's Tame Bears

(c. 1914)—Theodore Roosevelt

"The bears get so bold that they barge into the kitchen."

Warning signs used to read, "Bears Will Eat Candy and Fingers Right Off Your Hands." Despite regulations forbidding bear feeding, many people did it to entice the animals for close-up views. And the bears obliged by leaning next to car windows to beg for treats and parading their cubs. Although "bear jams" sometimes blocked traffic for miles, most people figured that was just a price that had to be paid to see their antics. It seemed normal to President Theodore Roosevelt too. Here's how he described Yellowstone bears about 1914.

It was amusing to read the proclamations addressed to the tourists by the park management, in which they were solemnly warned that the bears were really wild animals, and that they must on no account be either fed or teased. It is curious to think that the descendants of the great grizzlies which were the dread of the early explorers and hunters should now be semi-domesticated creatures, boldly hanging around crowded hotels for the sake of what they can pick up, and quite harmless so long as any reasonable precaution is exercised. They are much safer, for instance, than any ordinary dairy bull or stallion, or even ram, and, in fact, there is no danger from them at all unless they are encouraged to grow too familiar or are in some way molested.

Of course, among the thousands of tourists, there is a percentage of thoughtless and foolish people; and when such people go out in the afternoon to look at the bears feeding they occasionally bring themselves into jeopardy by some senseless act. The black bears and the cubs of the bigger bears can readily be driven up trees, and some of the tourists occasionally do this. Most of the animals never think of resenting it; but now and then one is run across which has its feelings ruffled by the performance.

In the summer of 1902, the result proved disastrous to a too inquisitive tourist. He was traveling with his wife, and at one of the hotels, they went out toward the garbage pile to see the bears feeding. The only bear in sight was a large she, which, as it turned out, was in a bad temper because another party of tourists a few minutes before had been chasing her cubs up a tree. The man left his wife and walked toward the bear to see how close he could get. When he was some distance off, she charged him, whereupon he bolted back toward his wife. The bear overtook him, knocked him down and bit him severely. But the man's wife, without hesitation, attacked the bear with that thoroughly feminine weapon, an umbrella, and frightened her off. The man spent several weeks in the park hospital before he recovered.

Perhaps the following telegram sent by the manager of the Lake Hotel to Major Pitcher illustrates with sufficient clearness the mutual relations of the bears, the tourists, and the guardians of the public weal in the park. The original was sent me by Major Pitcher. It runs:

"Lake. 7-27-'03. Major Pitcher, Yellowstone: As many as seventeen bears in an evening appear on my garbage dump. Tonight eight or ten. Campers and people not of my hotel throw things at them to make them run away. I cannot, unless there personally, control this. Do you think you could detail a trooper to be there every evening from say six o'clock until dark and make people remain behind the danger line laid out by Warden Jones? Otherwise, I fear some accident. The arrest of one or two of these campers might help. My own guests do pretty well as they are told. James Barton Key. 9 a.m."

Major Pitcher issued the order as requested.

At times, the bears get so bold that they take to making inroads on the kitchen. One completely terrorized a Chinese cook. It would drive him off and then feast upon whatever was left behind. When a bear begins to act in this way or to show surliness it is sometimes necessary to shoot it. Other bears are tamed until they will feed out of the hand, and will come at once if called. Not only have some of the soldiers and scouts tamed bears in this fashion, but occasionally a chambermaid or waiter girl at one of the hotels has thus developed a bear as a pet.

This whole episode of bear life in Yellowstone is so extraordinary that it will be well worthwhile for any man who has the right powers and enough time, to make a complete study of the life and history of the Yellowstone bears. Indeed, nothing better could be done by some one of our outdoor faunal naturalists than to spend at least a year in Yellowstone, and to study the life habits of all the wild creatures therein. A man able to do this, and to write down accurately and interestingly what he had seen, would make a contribution of permanent value to our nature literature with their majestic beauty all unmarred.

— Excerpt from Theodore Roosevelt, "Wilderness Reserves," in George Bird Grinnell (ed.), *American Big Game in Its Haunts* (Harper: New York, 1914), 23–51.

PART 12:
TRAVELER ANTICS

INTRODUCTION

Yellowstone tourists have always found interesting ways to have fun.

Early Yellowstone travelers found lots of ways to entertain themselves. Of course, they spent a lot of time watching wildlife and marveling at natural wonders like geysers, canyons, and waterfalls. But there were other things to do, like playing practical jokes on companions and experimenting on geothermal features.

Travel by horse was slow, so people had ample time to get to know each other. That usually resulted in amicable relationships, but sometimes people played practical jokes on each other for fun, or to avenge transgressions.

Before park officials began enforcing rules, people could do pretty much whatever they wanted with natural features. Many tourists' accounts contain descriptions of such things as doing laundry in geysers, rolling boulders down canyons, and putting soap into geysers to force them to play.

Shooting Jake Smith's Hat

(1870)—N. P. Langford

While his companions try to demonstrate their prowess with pistols, a man sneaks in wellplaced rifle shots.

One of the members of the famous Washburn Expedition that explored the upper Yellowstone in 1870 was a jocular man named Jake Smith. Smith was always ready to gamble, but unfortunately he lost all his money in a card game the night before the trip started. Undaunted, Jake came up with a way to replenish his stake, losing his hat in the bargain. N. P. Langford tells the story.

Descending the range to the east, we reached Trail Creek, a tributary of the Yellowstone about 3 o'clock in the afternoon, where we are now camped for the night. We are now fairly launched upon our expedition without the possibility of obtaining outside assistance in case we need it. Our safety will depend upon our vigilance. We are all well armed with long range repeating rifles and needle guns, though there are but few of our party who are experts at off-hand shooting with a revolver.

In the course of our discussion Jake Smith expressed his doubt whether any member of our party is sufficiently skilled in the use of the revolver to hit an Indian at even a close range. He offered to put the matter to a test by setting up his hat at a distance of twenty yards for the boys to shoot at with their revolvers, without a rest, at twenty-five cents a shot.

Several members of our party blazed away with indifferent success—with the result that Jake was adding to his exchequer without damage to his hat. I could not resist the inclination to quietly drop out of sight behind a clump of bushes. From my place of concealment I sent from my breech-loading Ballard repeating rifle four bullets in rapid succession, through the hat—badly riddling it.

Jake inquired, "Whose revolver is it that makes that loud report?" He did not discover the true state of the case, but removed the target with the ready acknowledgment that there were members of our party whose aim with a revolver was more accurate than he had thought.

— Excerpt from N. P. Langford, *Diary of the Washburn Expedition to the Yellowstone and Firehole Rivers in the Year 1870* (St. Paul, Minn.: J. E. Haynes, 1905), 6–8.

Teaching Greenhorns about Snipe Driving

(1872)—N. P. Langford

Old-timers have fun at the expense of new recruits.

The tradition of playing tricks on the naïve runs deep in the history of the northern Rockies. The famous Yellowstone explorer N. P. Langford told this story in his account of traveling with the second Hayden Expedition to Yellowstone Park in 1872.

Among our own hunters was a trapper named Shep Medary—a lively, roystering mountaineer, who liked nothing better than to get a joke upon any unfortunate "pilgrim" or "tenderfoot" who was verdant enough to confide in his stories of mountain life.

"What a night!" said Shep, as the moon rose broad and clear—"what a glorious night for drivin' snipe!"

Here was something new. Two of our young men were eager to learn all about the mystery.

"Driving snipe! What's that, Shep? Tell us about it."

"Did ye never hear?" replied Shep, with a face expressive of wonder at their ignorance. "Why, it's as old as the mountains, I guess; we always choose such weather as this for drivin' snipe. The snipe are fat now, and they drive better, and they're better eatin' too. I tell you, a breakfast of snipe, broiled on the buffalo chips, is not bad to take, is it, Dick?"

Beaver Dick, who had just arrived in camp, thus appealed to, growled an assent to the proposition contained in Shep's question; and the boys, more anxious than ever, pressed Shep for an explanation.

"Maybe," said one of them, "maybe we can drive the snipe tonight and get a mess for breakfast: what have we got to do, Shep?"

"Oh well," responded Shep, "if you're so plaguey ignorant, I'm afeard you won't do. Howsomever, you can try. You boys get a couple of them gunnysacks and candles, and we'll go out and start 'em up."

Elated with the idea of having a mess of snipe for breakfast, the two young men, under Shep's direction, each equipped with a gunnysack and candle, followed him out upon the plain, half a mile from camp, accompanied by some half-dozen members of our party. The spot was chosen because of its proximity to a marsh that was supposed to be filled with snipe. In reality it was the swarming place for mosquitoes.

"Now," said Shep, stationing the boys about ten feet apart, "open your sacks, be sure and keep the mouths of 'em wide open, and after we leave you, light your candles and hold 'em well into the sack, so that the snipe can see, and the rest of us will drive 'em up. It may take a little spell to get 'em started, but if you wait patiently they'll come."

With this assurance the snipe-drivers left them and returned immediately to camp.

"I've got a couple of green 'uns out there," said Shep with a sly wink. "They'll wait some time for the snipe to come up, I reckon."

The boys followed directions—the sacks were held wide open, the candles kept in place. There they stood, the easy prey of the remorseless mosquitoes. An hour passed away, and yet from the ridge above the camp the light of the candles could be seen across the plain. Shep now stole quietly out of camp, and, making a long circuit, came up behind the victims and, raising a war-whoop, fired his pistol in the air.

The boys dropped their sacks and started on a two-forty pace for camp, coming in amid the laughter and shouts of their companions.

— Excerpt from N. P. Langford, "The Ascent of Mount Hayden." *Scribner's Monthly*, 6, no. 2 (June 1873): 129–157.

Angering Old Faithful

(1877)—Frank Carpenter

Tourists dump rubble down the famous geyser just to find out what will happen.

Today most Yellowstone tourists believe that nature is fragile. They wouldn't collect a leaf or pick a flower for fear of causing irreparable damage. But early tourists shattered geological features to gather specimens, slaughtered animals for fun, and experimented with geysers.

On a Sunday in the summer of 1877, Frank Carpenter was lolling around Old Faithful with his companions: Dingee, Arnold, and Mr. Houston—and Frank's sisters, Ida and Emma. They soon tired of quietly observing the Sabbath and decided to experiment with Old Faithful. Here's Frank's story.

We conclude that we will do our washing, since such an opportunity for "boiling clothes" will not be presented again soon.

Emma and Ida put their clothes in a pillowcase. Dingee took off his blouse and tied a large stone in it and I finished tying it with my handkerchief. Arnold also removed his jacket—and we repaired to the laundry—Old Faithful.

We hear the preparatory rumbling and the waters rise a few feet above the surface. Mr. Houston now gives the command to throw our garments into the water. The water goes down and remains low so long that we begin to feel uneasy. Dingee begins to lament his loss and to curse the man who "put us up to the job."

Mr. Houston remarks that it will be all right, and the next instant, with a rush and a roar she "goes off." The clothes, mixed in every conceivable shape, shoot up to a distance of a hundred feet and fall with a splash in the basins below.

The water subsides, and we fish out the clothing, which, we find as nice and clean as a Chinaman could wash it with a week's scrubbing. Dingee rejoices.

Wishing to experiment further, we collect an immense quantity of rubbish and drop it into the crater. We fill it to the top with at least a thousand pounds of stones, trees, and stumps. Now we sit down to await further developments.

At the exact time advertised, sixty-five minutes from the time of the last eruption, the earth begins to tremble. We hear the rush again. "Off she goes," and away go rocks, trees and rubbish—to a height of seventy-five or eighty feet.

Old Faithful seems to have been angered by the unwarrantable procedure on our parts—or he wishes to show us that our attempts to check his power are futile. And he furnishes entertainment of unusual magnitude and duration.

— From Frank D. Carpenter, *The Wonders of Geyserland: A Trip to Yellowstone National Park* (Black Earth, Wis., Burnett & Son, 1878), 33–34.

Rolling Boulders down Gardner Canyon

(1885)—George W. Wingate

An angler yells as huge rocks tumble toward him.

In the summer of 1885, General George W. Wingate took his wife and daughter through Yellowstone Park. Although the system of roads was complete by then, the Wingates and his companions decided to make their tour on horseback, the better to see the sights. The general, who was a Civil War veteran and later president of the National Rifle Association, wrote a charming book about his adventures in the park. Here's an excerpt.

The 19th being Sunday, the ladies rested in camp, while I took our three men and rode to the Middle Falls of the Gardner. There was no road; merely a blazed trail through the woods, which we had to hunt up. This involved fording the river and considerable skirmishing among fallen timber, and in and out of places where I would never have dreamed of venturing on horseback in the East. Finally, the trail (probably an old elk runway) was found. It was just wide enough for a horse to get through, and led us up the mountain by a comparatively easy grade, but along a precipice, with yawning depths, to glance into which was sometimes quite startling. But we were rapidly becoming accustomed to that sort of thing and took it as naturally as our ponies did.

After a steady climb of four miles, we found ourselves on the edge of a canyon overlooking the falls. It was a magnificent and most picturesque sight. Mr. Winson's very accurate guidebook gives the depth of the canyon at from 1,200 to 1,500 feet. I think this is an error as this would be deeper than the Great Canyon (which the same authority gives at 1,200 feet) and I should think the latter was considerably the deepest. But whatever the measurement, it is of appalling depth, about 500 yards wide at the top and very narrow at the bottom, not to exceed 150 feet. The sides drop from the brink above in almost perpendicular ledges, as steep as the Palisades on the Hudson River and four times their depth. Into this cleft in the rocks, the river plunges in one unbroken fall of over a hundred feet and then continues its fall in a series of cascades to the bottom of the dark chasm. The white fall, the tumbling water, and the dark shadows of the canyon, make a striking picture.

After fully enjoying the scene, we amused ourselves by rolling large rocks over the cliff. It was wonderful to see a stone the size of a trunk leap into the air in a plunge of 200 or 300 feet, strike the shelf below as if thrown by a catapult, and with such tremendous force as to rebound twenty feet, and after a series of such terrific bounds, make another tremendous leap to the slope below, continuing in bound after bound until it reached the creek, growing smaller and smaller at each movement until it seemed no larger than a football.

While indulging in this boyish sport a faint shout came up from below signifying that there was someone down in the canyon. It is unnecessary to say that we at once stopped the stone rolling. Looking down we saw a party of fishermen from the hotel dodging up the bottom of the canyon with great celerity and evident anxiety as to whether any more stones might be expected. So great was the depth that they looked like children.

While watching them, Horace's hat blew off and lodged in the shelf at the foot of the cliff at the brink of which we were standing. It seemed only a short way down, and we undertook to fasten the picket ropes of the horses together so as to aid him to descend, but found they would not begin to reach the distance. Horace was determined to have his hat, and with regular western recklessness started to climb down.

By selecting places where the fragments from the sides of the canyon had formed a slope, and clinging to the trees and shrubs, he managed to work his way to the shelf below, and up on that to his beloved headgear. He had to go so far down that he appeared only half his natural size.

The exploit was more hazardous than we imagined. Mr. Davis, of the Northern Pacific Railroad, as I was afterwards told, undertook to climb up near that very spot only a day or two before. The loose stone slid under his feet, as is common in mountain climbing, but which, though fatiguing, is not dangerous if one keeps moving. Finally, he climbed out on a large boulder, the size of a small house, to look around. Suddenly he discovered that it too was in motion. He slid along upon it for some distance expecting it would roll at every instant, when fortunately, it passed so near a tree that he was enabled to spring into the branches, while the boulder went crashing downwards for a thousand feet, snapping the trees like pipe stems in its course.

— From George Wood Wingate, *Through the Yellowstone Park on Horseback* (Judd and Judd: New York, 1886), 79–81.

Soaping Beehive Geyser to Make It Play

(1892)—Georgina Synge

"That night we sallied forth . . . armed with two large bars of Brown Windsor tied up in a pocket-handkerchief."

Apparently the practice of soaping geysers to make them erupt began in the 1880s after a concessionaire decided that the naturally agitating Chinaman Spring would be the perfect place to do laundry. After tossing in clothing, the concessionaire added soap and the spring erupted, spewing clothing over the landscape.

Soon tourists began stripping soap off of store shelves and taking it from hotel bathrooms so they could eliminate the tedium of waiting for geysers to play. Of course officials soon banned the practice, but it was hard to control. Here's Georgina Synge's description of a clandestine soaping of Beehive Geyser.

The geyser we set our hearts on seeing was the "Beehive" just opposite our camp, the other side of the basin. The cone, which really has all the appearance of a beehive in the distance, is about three feet in height and is beautifully coated with beaded silica. Its action is different to any other geyser, as the water is projected with such force from its comparatively small vent-hole, that it goes up in one perfectly straight pillar to over two hundred feet; and, instead of falling in floods on each side like the others, seems to evaporate into wreaths of steam and vapor.

Now there is a sure and almost certain method for inducing a geyser to play out of its accustomed hours, and this is done by what is called "soaping" them! It may sound incredible, but it is a well known fact (which we attested on several occasions) that a bar or two of common yellow soap, cut up into pieces and slipped into a geyser cone, will have the desired effect in a very short interval. This is supposed to be partly caused by the soap creating a film on the water, which prevents the steam escaping. Smithson was as keen as we were that the Beehive should play. He assured us he had seen it soaped over and over again, with the most brilliant results.

So that night we sallied forth after all the world had gone to bed, armed with two large bars of Brown Windsor tied up in a pocket-handkerchief. The moon was shining fitfully behind the clouds, and now and then gleamed forth upon us, as, having crossed the river, we climbed up the white sloping sides of the Beehive.

It was not due to play for several days, and as we peered down its dark funnel-like orifice, we could hear a soft peaceful gurgling, but nothing more; and even this quite ceased after we had slipped in the soap. We sat down then and watched. Presently it began to boil up—little by little—with a buzzing sort of noise as if it were hard at work. Every now and then it threw up a few squirts of water, and Smithson, who was getting very excited, laid his bottom dollar it was going to play. But, alas, though it seemed to be trying with all its might, yet it never quite got off, and having watched for nearly an hour, we decided to send Smithson back to camp for some more soap.

Perhaps we had not put in enough, we thought, though Smithson assured us two bars was all it had ever wanted before. Well, in went the second lot, but with just the same result. It showed all the premonitory symptoms, boiled over, made a few gasps, and sent up a few small jets, and then gave it up. We got quite desperate at last. It was nearly twelve o'clock, and very cold, as a sharp frost had set in. We thought, however, we would have one more try.

We hurried back to camp. There we found Elijah, stretched fast asleep before the smoldering embers of the fire. We cruelly awoke him, and made him produce the last piece of yellow bar, which we had hitherto thought necessary to leave for washing purposes. And to augment this, A. insisted on my bringing forth our few and treasured cakes of Pears. But no, even this last sacrifice was of no avail—that Beehive would not play! Smithson was furious, the first time it had ever refused for him; someone must have soaped it the day before, and if only we would wait it was sure to begin soon. But we decided we could not freeze there all night, even to see the Beehive display; and so dejectedly we made our way once more back to camp. Just as we were going off to sleep we heard a roar—something was "guising" at last, but we were too tired to stir even if it had been "Excelsior." The next morning, however, just as we were dressed, we heard the roar again, like the sound of a sudden hurricane or of numberless distant guns. "She's off—the 'Beehive's guisin,'" shouted Smithson, and off we dashed, helter-skelter, arriving breathless, but in capital time to see a grand eruption.

It was terrific. It seemed as if the whole hillside must be blown out by the tremendous force with which it burst forth. Higher and higher it soared, in one great round perpendicular column of over two hundred feet, clouding the whole sky with masses of spray and steam. Presently a gust of wind blew up and carried the topmost wreaths in feathery masses over the valley, and we were able to stand quite close to lee of it without getting a drop upon us. It played for about twenty minutes, then wavered, trembled, and finally subsided with sundry gurgles and groans. As we came away, several people who had hurried out from their beds to see the sight began making remarks on the curious fact of the Beehive playing before its proper time. "That's been soaped," said a man who belonged to the place, looking suspiciously round, at which we appeared innocently surprised.

— Excerpt from Georgina M. Synge, "Geyser-Land," *A Ride Through Wonderland* (Sampson, Marston & Company: London, 1892), 48–70.

The Army Protects Theodore Roosevelt

(1903)—Henry Harrison Lewis

*A snoopy reporter attempts to intrude
on the president's trip to the park.*

*When the US Congress established Yellowstone National Park in 1872, they put
civilians in charge, but didn't appropriate enough money for the job of protecting it.
Poachers decimated wildlife, collectors vandalized natural features, and monopo-
lists gouged travelers. Things became so bad by 1886 that the US Army was asked
to step in. It ran the park until 1918, when the National Park Service took over.*

*By all accounts the army was diligent and left its mark in ways ranging from
the shape of rangers' hats to the Grand Loop pattern of roadways. Here's a story
that describes how effectively they protected President Theodore Roosevelt from an
intrepid reporter named Henry Lewis.*

An incident that occurred during President Roosevelt's recent visit proves
the exceedingly careful manner in which the park is guarded. When Mr.
Roosevelt made it known that his object in entering the Yellowstone Park
was to secure several days of complete privacy, and that he did not want any
one aside from Major Pitcher and the picked escort to accompany him, a
certain correspondent representing a New York daily, who had been ordered
to be on hand in case of any accident to the president or other emergency of
national importance, resolved to ignore the president's request and to follow
him at all hazards.

With this object in view, he attempted to bribe some of the native population, but without success. Not disheartened by his failure to secure a friendly
companion and guide, the correspondent hired a horse and persuaded a stray
dog to accompany him. This was on the afternoon of the president's arrival at
Fort Yellowstone. The fort is five miles from Gardiner, where the rest of the
correspondents and the president's party had stopped.

The recreant correspondent set forth in high glee at the possibility of working a "beat" on his fellow-craftsmen. As he rode along through the leafy lanes and past the towering cliffs, which in part line the road to the springs, he felt very well satisfied with himself, and chuckled at the ease with which he had evaded the guards stationed near Gardiner. Suddenly, as he was entering a particularly dark part of a forest, he heard a voice from the brush on the right.

"Theodore Jones," it said slowly and in unmistakable authoritative tones. "Theodore Jones!"

The correspondent reined up his horse in amazement. Who was it calling his name? Had he been followed from Gardiner? If so, why did the voice come from the bushes and evidently some distance from the road?

"Hello!" he shouted, in reply.

There was no answer. He called again and again, but without result. Then he put spurs to his horse and rode on. Half a mile further down the road, just as he was passing through another bit of woodland, a deep voice called out seemingly at his very elbow:

"Theodore Jones! Theodore Jones-s-s! Better go back."

For one moment, the newspaperman hesitated, then he rode resolutely forward. He felt that he was being tricked, but he intended to see the game out. He was a bit nervous because he realized that his course of action was not entirely honorable, and it was with something very like relief that he espied at a turn in the road a United States trooper sitting with horse blocking the path and a rifle slung carelessly across the pommel of his saddle.

"Halt" called out the soldier. "Mr. Jones, you are wanted at headquarters."

"How do you know my name is Jones?" demanded the correspondent.

The trooper smiled as if the question was a joke. Placing one hand upon the correspondent's bridle, he led him without further words to Fort Yellowstone. A technical charge of unlawfully bringing a dog into the reservation was entered against Mr. Jones, but he was released on his promise not to enter the park again until the president's return. The incident had its value in showing the extreme care taken by the park's guardians in keeping out unwelcome visitors. The correspondent's errand was known at Headquarters before he had crossed the line.

— Excerpt from Henry Harrison Lewis, "Managing a National Park," *The Outlook* 74, no. 18 (Aug. 29, 1903): 1036–1040.

Having Fun at the Handkerchief Pool

(1903)—Hester Ferguson Henshall

A fish biologist's wife describes tourists washing their hankies in a hot spring.

The Handkerchief Pool was one of the most popular geothermal features in Yellowstone Park in 1903 when Hester Henshall visited the park with her husband, angling writer and fish biologist Dr. James Henshall. A few years later the pool quit working, apparently because it was jammed by debris thoughtless tourists had dumped into it. In the Henshall's tour group was Lillian Elhert, an intrepid young woman who always thrust herself into the middle of things. Here's Hester's description of Miss Lillian's antics at the Handkerchief Pool.

The Handkerchief Pool reminded one of a great pot of boiling water, seething, roaring and bubbling, and issuing clouds of steam with a washday odor. Miss Lillian Ehlert must put her handkerchief in the pool, of course. We gathered round to watch it. It floated awhile, circling the pool, then suddenly disappeared down a sucking eddy, out of sight.

We watched and waited, some of us thinking it had gone forever, but at last it popped up in another part of the pool and floated once more to the surface. It was then taken out with a stick, to be gazed upon by all of the party with something akin to awe. We wondered where it had been when lost to sight—what it had seen underground, and what tale it could tell if gifted with speech.

Miss Ehlert simply said: "No checky no washee, but I got it all the same."

— Excerpt from the journal of Hester Ferguson Henshall, *Trip Through Yellowstone National Park 1903,* Montana Historical Society Archives.

The handkerchief pool where travelers could launder their dainties used to be one of Yellowstone's most popular geothermal features. NATIONAL PARK SERVICE

Maud Gets Her Revenge

(1913)—L. Louise Elliott

A camp cook gets even with a supercilious guest.

In 1913 Louise Elliott published a book about a young schoolteacher from Lander, Wyoming, who took a job as a camp assistant for a mobile camp tour. In her preface Elliott confesses that she used several techniques that critics now might label "new journalism." She created composite characters by combining traits of her camp companions, and made up a "little romance" for her protagonist.

We can forgive Elliott because she provided an explicit disclaimer—and an entertaining portrait of travel to Yellowstone Park in the early twentieth century. While her tales must be taken with the proverbial grain of salt, we probably can take her word that "the camp episodes and jokes, the weather and scenery, and the statistics" were all accurate descriptions copied from her diary.

Elliott gives interesting details of her trip: a cook who makes biscuits "charred on the outside and doughy in the middle;" a guide who carries "the scratchiest flannels" to be worn by anyone who didn't heed his warning to bring warm clothing; and snobbish hotel guests who refuse to return the greetings of lowly campers.

At one point during the story, Elliott says her protagonist, Violet, and her friend, Maud, became irritated with one of their guests—a Boston lady that they called "the Spinster." Here's Louise's story about that.

Maud and I baked enough biscuits for supper and some cup cakes while the Spinster complained of all the discomforts of camp life as compared with her home conveniences. Neither did she forget to mention her lovely twenty-eight dollar and fifty-cent air mattress.

"That settles it once for all," whispered Maud. "Never again!"

Well Maud had her revenge—and not once today has the Spinster boasted of her comfortable pneumatic mattress. I wondered last night why Maud was anxious to retire early as she is usually the last one to bed.

The great pine fire was lighting our tent, and the Spinster was peacefully enjoying her first snore when I saw our Irish lassie get stealthily out of bed—and crawl over to the hated mattress. She certainly must have made a thorough study of the mechanism—she knew just where to find the valve screw. She gave a few turns—crept back into bed again—and began breathing hard and steady.

Maud had not let me into her proposed vengeance because she feared I would not countenance it. But I suspected that the air was slowly leaking out of the mattress under the sleeping Bostonian. Soon that lady stopped her regular breathing and sat up in bed. She began fumbling under her and muttered, "Well, I never." Finally she got up, punching the mattress, muttering something and reached into her bag.

Pump, pump, pump—I tried so hard to keep from giggling that a snort escaped from my throat. Maud began to talk incoherently and to toss and throw her arms about to cover my telltale noises. "No sir, I told you before that I will not dance—no—no—." Then her voice died away and she snored vociferously while the—*pump, pump, pump*—continued. At last the wonderful pneumatic was restored to its proper stage of plumpness and the weary Spinster was soon resuming her snores where she left off.

She was more silent than usual this morning and did not allude in any way to her mattress. But while Maud and I were doing up the dishes, she went into the tent and gave her bed a thorough examination. She became more talkative after she had read the little pamphlet of directions, which had been attached to the mattress. After that she told the party how Maud had discussed her secrets and love affairs in her sleep.

Maud asked innocently, "What did I talk about?"

—Abridged from L. Louise Elliott, *Six Weeks on Horseback Through Yellowstone Park* (Rapid City, S.D.: *Rapid City Journal*, 1913), 73–75.

ABOUT THE AUTHOR

M. Mark Miller is a fifth-generation Montanan who grew up on a ranch in southwest Montana about ninety miles from Yellowstone Park. His interest in early park travel began when he was a little boy listening to his grandmother's tales of cooking bread in hot springs and throwing red flannel underwear into geysers to tint their next eruption pink.

WINSLOW STUDIO

He worked for Montana newspapers while in college at the University of Montana. After graduating, he was a reporter and editor for newspapers in Utah and Kentucky. He earned a doctorate and became a journalism professor at the Universities of Wisconsin and Tennessee.

Miller returned home to Montana in 2003. He has been researching Yellowstone Park history since then and has a collection of more than four hundred first-person accounts of park travel before 1923. Globe Pequot Press published his book, *Adventures in Yellowstone: Early Travelers Tell Their Tales*, in 2009.

Miller's articles on Yellowstone Park and Montana history have appeared in the *Montana Quarterly, Big Sky Journal* and the *Pioneer Museum Quarterly*. He is seeking a publisher for his middle-grade novel about a fourteen-year-old boy's adventures in Yellowstone Park in 1871, and is working on a narrative history of the encounters between the Nez Perce Indians and tourists in Yellowstone Park in 1877.

He lives in Bozeman, where he volunteers at the Pioneer Museum. Miller presents a program, "Sidesaddles and Geysers: Women's Adventures in Early Yellowstone," for the Humanities Montana Speakers Bureau.